JD VANCE
and the FUTURE *of the* REPUBLICAN PARTY

JD VANCE
and the FUTURE *of the* REPUBLICAN PARTY

FRANK DeVITO

Published by Bombardier Books
An Imprint of Post Hill Press
ISBN: 979-8-89565-369-2
ISBN (eBook): 979-8-89565-370-8

JD Vance and the Future of the Republican Party
© 2026 by Frank DeVito
All Rights Reserved

Cover Design by Cody Corcoran

This is a work of nonfiction. All people, locations, events, and situations are portrayed to the best of the author's memory.

This book, as well as any other Bombardier Books publications, may be purchased in bulk quantities at a special discounted rate. Contact orders@bombardierbooks.com for more information.

No part of this book may be reproduced, stored in a retrieval system, or transmitted by any means without the written permission of the author and publisher.

Post Hill Press, LLC
New York • Nashville
posthillpress.com

Published in the United States of America
1 2 3 4 5 6 7 8 9 10

I dedicate this book to my dear wife Molly—
my greatest conversational partner and most
exacting editor—and to my five children.

CONTENTS

Foreword xi

I	Introduction 1	
II	Moving On Up: The Life of JD Vance 9	
III	Insights from *Hillbilly Elegy* 23	
	What It Takes to Achieve the American Dream Is Not Simply Wealth or Intelligence 24	
	America's Problem Is Primarily One of Class and Culture, Not Race 28	
	The Fallout of a Deindustrialized America 31	
	Conservative Politics Moving Forward 33	
	A Man Like Us 37	
IV	Vance's Early Political Writings 41	
	JD Vance: Obama Fan? 42	
	Vance Goes Home to Ohio 46	
V	Vance and the Poisoned Garden of America 53	
VI	Vance Comes Around to Trump 65	
	Vance Against Trump 66	
	What if Trump is Right? 69	

VII	Beyond Libertarianism 79	
	What Is Libertarianism and Why Does It Matter? .. 80	
	JD Vance: Beyond Libertarianism 81	
	The Health of America... 87	
VIII	A New Conservatism: Workers and Families................ 93	
	Vance the Senate Candidate: New Role,	
	Same Priorities.. 103	
IX	A Pro-Life Messaging Problem................................... 115	
	The Pro-Life Movement Must Learn	
	Incrementalism in the Face of Reality 119	
	The Problem of Active Support.............................. 121	
	Finding a Delicate Balance..................................... 122	
X	Vance the Politician 125	
	The Vance Orbit: Donors, Intellectuals,	
	Political Operatives... 126	
	Political Operatives... 129	
	Practical Politics: How to Win Elections 132	
	Vance the Tactical Politician................................... 135	
XI	Vance the Legislator... 141	
	English Language Unity Act 142	
	Financial Regulatory Accountability Act of 2023 .. 145	
	A Bill to Restrict the Chinese Government 146	
	The FAUCI Act 148	
	The Dismantle DEI Act... 150	
	Ukraine Aid Transparency Act 151	
	Illegal Immigration Bills 152	
	Conclusion: A Legislative Roadmap for	
	the Future... 155	
XII	Vance the Catholic Convert.. 157	
	Vance the Catholic Convert................................... 159	

	Vance the Catholic VP	170
XIII	Towards a New Republican Party	177
	Vance and the Foreign Policy of the New Republican Party	177
	Domestic Policy	183
	Pro-Family Policy	185
	Workers and Manufacturing	188
	Personnel	192
XIV	Conclusion: The Future of the Republican Party Under President Vance?	195

Acknowledgments	203
About the Author	205

FOREWORD

Had Frank DeVito written a book on "the future of the Republican Party" in 1988, it would have comprised a single chapter with seven words: "more or less, more of the same." While George H.W. Bush campaigned on a "a kinder, gentler conservatism" than that of his predecessor, he ascended to the presidency on the promise of a third Reagan term.

Mr. DeVito might have recycled the same manuscript in the leadup to the subsequent five presidential elections: Bob Dole, George W., John McCain, and Mitt Romney colored their campaigns with their respective personalities, but their platforms remained consistent: tax cuts, migration, free trade, and a rising tide of global liberalism that would lift all ships, flatten the world, and end history.

After 2016, the copy editors for such a book would have faced the tedious task of swapping tenses, as the future suddenly became the past. The Trump-Pence campaign kept the tax cuts but seemed to ditch just about every other tenet of Republican Party orthodoxy, embracing protective tariffs, immigration restriction, foreign policy restraint, and a focus on family policy and the restoration of communities hollowed out by globalization.

Though lambasted as heretical by the Republican establishment, these policies represented less a revolution than a return to the positions that the party had traditionally held. Abraham Lincoln, the first Republican president, famously declared, "Give us a protective tariff, and we shall have the greatest nation on earth." Calvin Coolidge signed the restrictive Immigration Act of 1924. No less a conservative than William F. Buckley Jr. supported the America First Committee's campaign against American involvement in the Second World War.

With the election of Trump, everything old was new again. But the winning ticket reflected the tensions of this intra-party about-face. The President attracted new voters with *avant-garde* prescriptions and tactics; the Vice President assuaged the party's old guard with the sort of stable presence and rhetoric to which it had grown accustomed. But the political visions were diverging and formally split in 2024, when President Trump replaced the letters "p" and "e" with "v" and "a" on his bumper stickers. If Trump-Pence signaled a transition within the Republican Party, Trump-Vance confirmed a new course.

As Frank DeVito meticulously depicts, JD Vance embodied the zeitgeist: a working-class hero from a broken home in flyover country who knew that it would take more than bromides to resuscitate the American Dream for communities that decades of liberal globalism had left deracinated and despairing.

Had Vance's rhetoric appealed merely to the logos, he might have made a fine podcaster or think-tank scholar. What impelled his meteoric political rise has more to do with ethos and pathos. Vance understood all too well the political disorder that results from neglect of the family. Raised vaguely Evangelical and then irreligious, he appreciated with the surprise of St. Augustine the divine "Beauty, ever ancient, ever new." As an alum of the nation's most prestigious law school as well as the rarefied worlds of corporate law and venture capital, Vance saw firsthand the decadence and corruption of America's elite institutions. He could speak with not only authority and precision but also passion—even the zeal of a convert—on the issues of the moment.

Whether or not one supports the Vance vision, as Mr. DeVito does, matters little. What DeVito ultimately describes is not the Republican Party's future but its present. To ignore it is to risk irrelevance.

Michael Knowles
Nashville, Tennessee
October 7, 2025

I

Introduction

Who is JD Vance? And why does it matter? Before 2016, Vance was completely unknown to the American public. He already had a compelling life story. A poor kid from a dysfunctional family in Middletown, Ohio, encouraged by the loving support of his grandmother and a handful of others within his family and community, rises from a broken home and a broken community, joins the Marines, goes to Yale Law School, and ends up an elite lawyer working in Silicon Valley with some of the richest and smartest people in the world. It is an impressive and motivational story to show people that the rags-to-riches achievement of the American dream is still possible today.

While Vance's story is impressive, many such stories go untold. But something extraordinary happened. In 2016, Vance published his book *Hillbilly Elegy*—part memoir, part cultural commentary on the plight of ordinary working-class families and communities in America. That same year, the book was put into the hands of the conservative author Rod Dreher. Dreher saw a crucial analysis of middle America's citizens and voters who have been left behind by the American elites for too long. Dreher realized that "these people were invisible to the elite media…JD Vance gave them dignity."[1] The book came out just as Trump would capture this voting block of forgotten Americans, win the presidency in 2016, and transform US politics.

Dreher, aware of the populist uprising that was taking place and seeing the greatest explanation for this political moment in Vance's book, interviewed Vance for an article at *The American Conservative*.[2] The interview went viral; the *American Conservative* website crashed; *Hillbilly Elegy* quickly became a runaway bestseller. All of a sudden, JD Vance was a public figure on the national stage.

From that moment, Vance has been a star on the rise. He left Silicon Valley and returned to his native state of Ohio, now with connections to many rich and powerful people who saw his potential. After a couple years working in Ohio, he executed on a brilliant political strategy to win a crowded and competitive primary election to run for US Senate in Ohio. In 2022, at the age of thirty-eight and having never held political office, JD Vance became a US Senator.

---

[1] Joakim Scheffer, "The Man Who 'Made' JD Vance—Rod Dreher Featured in Danube Institute's New Podcast," *Hungarian Conservative*, April 30, 2025, https://www.hungarianconservative.com/articles/culture_society/jd-vance-rod-dreher-danube-institute-live-not-by-lies-premiere/.

[2] Rod Dreher, "Trump: Tribune of Poor White People," *The American Conservative*, July 22, 2016, https://www.theamericanconservative.com/trump-us-politics-poor-whites/.

During his brief time in the Senate, Vance quickly became the leading voice on the Right against continuing US aid to the war in Ukraine. This was about more than a particular war. There had long been a current on the Right that was skeptical of the neoconservative preference for heavy-handed interventions in foreign conflicts that are not directly in the American interest. Vance helped lead the way to a new conversation about foreign policy realism, ushering in the beginning of a new era within the Republican Party.

Then, in 2024, Vance once again overcame the political odds, beat out a crowded field, and was selected to run for Vice President of the United States. A few months later, at barely forty years old, this young man with the American dream story from Middletown, Ohio became the third-youngest vice president in American history.

It is not merely Vance's political office, but what he has done with it, that makes him stand out. He spent years developing the case for a new emphasis within domestic policy in the Republican Party. The new emphasis was not based primarily on the good of big business or the wealthy, but on the American family and the American worker. Vance laments that the concept of the American dream has been too focused on material wealth, on each generation having the opportunity to be better credentialed and wealthier than the previous generation. Vance reorients the American dream into a dream that will make most ordinary Americans happy and fulfilled. The new American dream depends on a nation in which as many people as possible have the opportunity to get married, have a stable marriage, raise children, and find meaningful work to support their families. This vision of the American dream is at the heart of the realignment of the Republican Party that is currently underway. Vance's own story, his analysis in *Hillbilly Elegy*, and his political writings over the last decade give him a keen insight and a strong passion for this realignment of Republican politics around families and workers.

So why does JD Vance matter?

First of all, Trump chose JD Vance as his vice president. And remember, this was a bold choice. Often, presidential candidates will choose a VP to help "balance the ticket." Trump could have chosen a running mate from a swing state. He could have selected a black or Latino or Asian Republican in an effort to continue making inroads into minority voting demographics. He could have chosen a woman. Or if he chose none of those things, he could have at least chosen someone who kept his head down, wasn't controversial, and was viewed as a moderating force to balance the charismatic and somewhat bombastic personality of Trump. But Trump did no such thing. Sensing that Biden was extremely weak (Trump chose Vance before Biden was replaced as the Democratic candidate), Trump chose an outspoken, conservative, young white guy from reliably Republican Ohio. It is clear that Trump was not choosing someone that he needed to help him win, but someone Trump thought was young and had a bright future in the Republican Party. Vance is the heir apparent to be the next Republican candidate for president in 2028.

But Vance is not worth writing about simply because he may be the next president. In many ways, the Republican Party is at a pivotal point. For over twenty years, the GOP had developed certain priorities: friendliness to big business and corporate interests, focused more on tax breaks and deregulation than social issues, and hawkish on excursionary foreign policy. When Trump came on the scene in 2015, he identified the ways in which a globalized view of politics had skewed politicians' priorities away from what was good for ordinary Americans. While Trump brought more of a gut intuition than a developed policy platform, he identified a core political problem very similar to the problem Vance identified in *Hillbilly Elegy*. This shift set off a realignment, a process where the wealthy and formally educated have migrated to the Democratic Party while working-class Americans have become the Republican base.

Vance identified the changes taking place in American political life early on in the process. He understands the root causes of family, community, and economic breakdown. He has written extensively on these various political, cultural, and religious topics for a decade. Regardless of who the next president will be, Vance's thought is key to understanding what a realigned, post-Trump Republican Party will look like.

Vance is the thought leader needed for this shift in priority for the Republican Party after Trump. And because Vance has been so prolific, we have an intellectual trail to follow. When writing a profile of a popular politician, one usually doesn't have much more to go on than campaign speeches and television interviews. But Vance has written widely, publishing essays everywhere from the *American Conservative* to the *New York Times*. He has spoken candidly about his own evolving views of American society and government institutions. He has reflected deeply on religion in America, on familial and cultural breakdown, on the effects of a globalized economy on American towns, and on the creative policies needed to focus American politics on the family and the worker. Rarely has such a shrewd and successful politician also been such an insightful public intellectual. If we want to know what Vance thinks about the most important issues that affect this country, we have a wide array of Vance's own writings to examine, many of which were written candidly, before he was ever running for office.

So the appeal of JD Vance is not only that he may very well be our next president. He is also a personally and politically fascinating person. He is much more interesting than the average politician. Vance is a brilliant writer, thinker, and public speaker. He is quick-witted and fun to listen to. He has an amazing personal story of overcoming adversity, going from a poor kid of humble hillbilly stock, through Yale Law School and Silicon Valley, to Vice President of the United States. And unlike many naturally brilliant and talented intellectuals, Vance is a very clever politician. He doesn't let the philosophical ideals and principles in which he has immersed himself over the last decade prevent him from being a prudent, practical man of action. He has the rare ability to think deeply about important things, and then translate those thoughts into policy and practical action.

For all these reasons, Vance is worth studying as a model statesman and the best hope of continuing to reshape the Republican Party in a post-Trump political world. This book seeks to show that Vance is a talented and fascinating individual, that he will likely be an important part of the future of the Republican Party after Trump, and that Conservatives should support him to lead the party after Trump.

***

Before moving into the substance of this book, a quick note about the timeline of Vance's public writing and speaking is worth adding. JD Vance officially declared his candidacy for the US Senate seat in Ohio on July 1, 2021. Unfortunately, there is no way to draw a clear line between ideas and writings articulated by a

JD Vance who had no political aspirations and those that were written or spoken with a campaign in mind.

Vance said repeatedly between 2016 and 2020 that he was not particularly interested in elected office, that he thought his talents might be used better elsewhere. It is up to the reader to decide how much political ambition may be present in any writings or speeches that were published by Vance prior to 2021.

It is not as simple as declaring that Vance never spoke with political ambition in mind or never aimed his public speech at his future political career. Vance is clearly an extremely talented, successful, and ambitious man. It is plausible that he did not explicitly have his sights set on public office when he was writing op-eds and essays in the years immediately after he wrote *Hillbilly Elegy*. There is evidence to support this position. In his early writings in 2016–2017, Vance took positions on policy issues (and made comments about public figures like Barack Obama and Donald Trump) that an aspiring Republican politician probably would never have published. There is reason to take Vance at his word and assume that, especially in his earlier essays, he was speaking candidly about how he views politics and culture. This is useful knowledge as we seek to understand the political mind of JD Vance.

Vance clearly knew he was talented, that he was in the public eye, and that he could leverage his fame for public ends. So the reader should be aware that, while the early writings are not campaign speeches or pieces written by a candidate, it is quite likely that Vance already knew in 2016 that he was shaping his public political image, wherever that would take him. When this book quotes extensively from a particular essay or speech, I will attempt to provide the year it was published so the reader can determine where the piece fits into the various stages of Vance's political life.

It is a unique opportunity to penetrate so deeply into the mind of a likely presidential candidate. A prominent politician rarely publishes thoughtful work on politics, culture, and religion years before running for office. As we continue to watch JD Vance rise in politics and take an increasingly important role in American public life, this book offers the reader the opportunity to understand how JD Vance views individuals, communities, politics, the proper role of government, and many of the most important issues of our day. Campaign speeches these days don't reveal too much about what candidates really think. This book can give a better, deeper insight into the mind of this great American man than one can ever acquire by following the news cycle.

Who is JD Vance? *Hillbilly Elegy* provides the reader with Vance's early life story. This book goes beyond that story and provides an in-depth look at who Vance is as a thinker, a writer, and a politician.

Why does it matter? Because Vance may very well be our next president. But even more because, regardless of office, Vance and those with whom he surrounds himself are at the center of the ongoing realignment taking place within the Republican Party. What Vance says and does about these political issues will affect the course of American politics for years, perhaps even decades, to come.

II

Moving On Up: The Life of JD Vance

Vance's own life story, while not the central theme of this book, tells a lot about both how he came to his political views and why he is so interesting to the American people. Vance does not come from a political dynasty or from a "successful" family. The basic outline of Vance's biography is well known through his own telling in *Hillbilly Elegy* as well as from his time on the campaign trail. Still, a bit of biographical background is fitting here. Not everyone has read *Hillbilly Elegy* or followed Vance as closely as I have. *Hillbilly Elegy* focuses on Vance's childhood and coming of age, with briefer sections on his time in the US Marine Corps, at Ohio State, and at Yale Law School. But that story still leaves a gap of several years between the end of his autobiography and the present day. While this book intends to be an intellectual profile about Vance and the future of the Republican Party rather than a biography, a brief biographical sketch will help contextualize how Vance has come to think about politics, government, America, and the current state of affairs by showing where he came from and where he has gone in his life.

JD Vance was born in Middletown, Ohio on August 2, 1984. But it is clear that his origin story starts in Jackson, Kentucky, not in Ohio. In *Hillbilly Elegy*, Vance talks about his family lineage as "hillbilly royalty." His family traces its ancestry to the member of the Kentucky Hatfield family whose act of murder started off the famous Hatfield-McCoy feud. He comes from a long line of Kentucky hillbillies that he deeply admired as a child. They were a family of proud, often violent people of Scots Irish descent. Vance's ancestry says a lot about where he comes from. He deeply identifies with the Appalachian hillbilly culture. Further, this ancestry says a lot about Vance's nuanced view of race and class. Vance highlights that the hillbillies of Scots Irish descent that make up his family have little in common with what is referred to as "white" American culture. Throughout his book, he continually points out that his people had much more in common culturally with southern black Americans than with white Americans. This insight speaks volumes about the overstated importance of "race" rather than class and culture in how people live and act.

Vance barely knew his biological father as a child, though they did reconnect later in his life. His mother was a volatile woman whose substance abuse and cycle of relationships led to a rather unstable childhood for Vance and his sister, Lindsay. He spent his childhood living with his mother at different houses with her various boyfriends and husbands. But it was chiefly his grandparents, his Papaw and especially his Mamaw, who raised him. His grandparents followed the migration of hillbillies from Kentucky to Ohio when they were young and newly married, seeking stable work and a better life. His grandparents' migration explains how he ended up an Ohioan.

The instability of having no regular father figure and an erratic mother led Vance to have the emotional trauma typical of a kid in such circumstances. He struggled with his grades, his weight, and forming healthy relationships. But beyond his individual struggles, living in a situation like this created a bigger societal problem. Vance was surrounded by people—both in his family and the greater community—who were living within unhealthy relationships and an economy where there were no examples of people rising up and achieving great things. This was the norm. Living in such a community leaves one with a certain hopelessness, with the sense that there is no way out, that there is nothing more to life than this. How can anyone be expected to rise out of poverty, to be a professional success and a good husband and father when he sees no examples of anyone else doing so?

Despite his absent father, numerous father figures, and an unstable mother, Vance was saved by the influence of a few people who showed him something else was possible. His Mamaw's influence cannot be overstated. Amid his mother's erratic living situations that presented ever-changing homes, husbands, and towns, Mamaw provided JD with stability. When his mother became out of control, JD could always go to Mamaw's house. When his mother's situation got worse, he went and lived with Mamaw full time. Yes, Mamaw was poor, sick, and swore like a sailor, but she gave him a stable place. The house was quiet. There was no domestic violence. There was food on the table. He was given a relatively calm space in which to do his homework, and he was told to do it. The benefit of a home that gives a child sufficient peace to study and play without shouting, fighting, or substance abuse cannot be overstated.

Beyond Mamaw's help, Vance benefited greatly from two examples in his family: his sister Lindsay and his Aunt Wee. His older sister was a stand-in mother for many years, and Aunt Wee was always kind and helpful. But their major contribution was simply that they married kind, stable men, had children, and didn't get divorced. This example from these two family members changed JD Vance's life. Vance returns to a constant theme in his writings: the American Dream is less about accumulating riches and more about the ability to be a good spouse, a good parent, and to have meaningful work to support a loving family. But, surrounded by familial dysfunction, Vance often worried that this normal, successful life was not attainable for him. Seeing Aunt Wee and then Lindsay settle down into happy family lives with good husbands changed Vance's world, because he now saw that this happy life was possible *for people like him*.

Another transformative experience Vance highlights is his time in the US Marine Corps. After high school, Vance began applying to colleges. He and Mamaw were desperately trying to figure out the application process and student loans when something dawned on him. His life thus far had not prepared him for success in the world beyond Middletown, Ohio. He wasn't even accustomed to waking up early or making his bed, let alone applying to college and managing his own finances. This realization that he simply was not ready for higher education led him to defer entrance into college and, with a mixed reaction from his family and disapproval from Mamaw, join the Marine Corps. This changed his life. The Marines taught him to wake up early, eat well, exercise, make his bed, learn how to get a loan, and responsibly manage finances. The Marines taught Vance lessons that should have been (but were not) learned in the family and the community. For the millions of children who grow up in a dysfunctional world like Vance did, an experience like the military can be the difference between continuing the pattern of dysfunction and learning the skills to rise up and escape a tragic cycle.

After the Marine Corps, Vance went to college at Ohio State as a man transformed. He woke up early, studied hard, excelled at his schoolwork while working several jobs, and got his first exposure to a world full of successful people. He succeeded in school, graduated with a good GPA, and applied to law school. Vance's account of why he went to law school again speaks to the effect his past had on his mentality. He really didn't know anything about the practice of law, but he knew that the only wealthy and successful people he knew in Middletown, Ohio were doctors and lawyers. He wanted to be successful but didn't want to work with blood, so he went to law school.

Vance refers to this decision as a great example of how difficult it is for lower class and working-class people to break into the middle and upper classes of society. They really don't understand how the whole thing works. It isn't that many of these folks don't have the intelligence or the ability to get professional degrees. They simply don't understand the ecosystem. They don't know what jobs are available in business, finance, law, policy, and so on. They don't know how to meet the people who have those jobs and can open their horizons to these unknown professional worlds. Carrying with him this profound ignorance of how the elite live, work, and network, Vance was accepted into Yale Law School, the most foreign environment he had ever experienced.

In a way, Vance had already risen out of his hillbilly community in Jackson, Kentucky and Middletown, Ohio. He went into the Marine Corps, deployed to Iraq, came back and went to Ohio State in Columbus to obtain his bachelor's degree. These experiences broadened his horizons, but they were nothing compared to the culture shock of Yale Law School. Many of the people he worked with in the military had working class, middle America backgrounds, just like him. Ohio State was a big, bustling, successful university, but it was an Ohio school with lots of Ohio kids. Yale Law was a different world altogether.

Yale Law made Vance realize that the world he had occupied in his life to that point and the world of the American elite were completely foreign to each other. Yes, Vance tells entertaining anecdotes about ordering chardonnay because he did not know how to pronounce sauvignon blanc and about not knowing why there were so many utensils at his place setting when he sat for the fanciest dinner he had ever attended. But the foreignness of the elite world went far beyond matters of upper-class tastes, manners, and customs. Vance realized that his classmates at Yale Law understood a different language and a different world because most of them had been raised by upper-class families, and most had attended Ivy League undergraduate institutions. They all knew which judges were "feeder" judges—judges where you obtained a clerkship because you then had a high likelihood of continuing on to a US Supreme Court clerkship. They understood the importance of getting on the Yale Law Review. They knew all about the different opportunities in big, prestigious law firms. Vance's classmates all seemed to know this intuitively from the first day they started classes. Vance was trying to navigate this world of elite legal education and career planning, but it felt like he was the only one navigating without a map.

In particular, Vance was unaware of the power of networking. *Hillbilly Elegy* often reminds the reader that very few people in Vance's community went to college, let alone to an elite college outside the state of Ohio. When a rare person rose up from Middletown, Ohio and became a professional success, the community would chalk it up to either natural brilliance, luck, or some combination of the two. Successful people were usually just assumed to be unusually smart. Vance had no idea about the power of networking. He didn't realize that the right recommendation from the right law professor could get your resume on the short list for a job. He didn't understand that the elite law professors at Yale wanted to get to know their students. He didn't know that showing up for office hours and getting to know these gatekeepers into the upper echelons of the legal profession could change the course of one's career. He knew that hard work and the right credentials mattered. But his time at Yale Law introduced him to the language, the customs, and the network that could open doors he didn't realize were available to him.

Vance's shocking experience at Yale Law is relevant for a number of reasons. As a personal story, it is an incredible triumph that he was able to move from the poor hillbilly community in which he grew up through Yale Law School—one of the most elite educational institutions in the world—to the highest ranks of society as a lawyer, venture capitalist, bestselling author, US senator, and now vice president of the United States.

Vance's cultural experience, especially at Yale, highlights the reason upward mobility is so difficult for the working class. It is not that ordinary, working-class people lack natural intelligence or access to a good education. What ordinary people lack is knowledge of the inside world of the elite: the power of networking, the path to land high-powered jobs through personal connections, and the ability to acquire and grow wealth that have little to do with one's W-2 paycheck. Many of these insights into the upper echelons of society are hidden from most ordinary Americans who did not grow up in that world, even the extremely bright and talented ones.

Finally, Vance's exposure to the elite and his ability to find mentors, to learn and grow through this extremely foreign and uncomfortable experience, explains how he got to where he is today. The same JD who was able to arrive at Yale Law School as a hillbilly Marine Corps veteran, overcome his discomfort, and learn to adapt to a different world, was able to translate this experience and succeed among the elites after his time at Yale Law. He journeyed into the equally foreign worlds of big law, venture capital, and US politics with the same sense. This was not where he grew up but it was possible to meet the right people, learn the right skills, and succeed despite the foreignness of the situation. Vance does not possess the typical pedigree of a successful national politician, which makes his story a model tale of the American Dream.

While this book is about the intellectual and political career of JD Vance, a biographical sketch would be incomplete without mentioning the importance of Vance's marriage to Usha Chilukuri, the daughter of academic parents who emigrated from India to California. Unlike Vance, Usha was born into the American cultural elite. She did her undergraduate studies at Yale, not Ohio State, and was quite comfortable among the high society into which Vance enculturated with great difficulty. But it is not Usha's background nor her accomplishments that are of primary interest here. Vance's marriage is relevant because, for him, it is the central accomplishment of his American Dream.

As Vance says often in his writings, the dream he had for a better life than his ancestors was not accumulation of wealth, credentials, and professional success. Rather, it was the ability to be a good husband and a good father, and to do meaningful work to support a stable, happy family. To accomplish this, Vance would need to escape the cycle of poverty, violence, and general dysfunction in which he grew up. When he met Usha, he fell in love with her almost instantly. She became his best friend, as well as a window into the familial world he dreamed of. Usha's family was kind, quiet, and stable. They didn't have explosive fights and they didn't speak badly about each other. In Usha, Vance found the opportunity to leave the cycle of family dysfunction he knew and to achieve the American Dream. Like Vance's sister and his Aunt Wee, Usha offered a glimpse into a better world, a vision of what was possible beyond his own experience.

It is also worth noting that Vance married Usha in 2014, a year after graduating law school and two years before *Hillbilly Elegy* was published. He did not marry Usha when he was already a public figure. Vance's marriage was not to acquire a trophy wife, a typical step for a politician to take. All the evidence points to the fact that he married Usha because they were deeply, genuinely in love and that they wanted to start a family together. Vance's marriage is a foundational aspect of his success, of his rise out of the life he knew as a child and into the life he wanted. The Vances have been happily married for over a decade and have three children together. Though Vance is now rising to the heights of politics, judging from his memoir and all his personal writings, he had already achieved the American dream before he ever entered the political arena.

Hillbilly Elegy covers the time from Vance's childhood through law school. He published the book three years after graduating from law school. The book says almost nothing about his post-law school life. Biographical details from the time Vance graduated from Yale Law to his run for US Senate, however, can be pieced together from other records and interviews.

After law school, Vance moved with Usha to Kentucky, where he clerked for a federal judge in the Eastern District of Kentucky for a year. This was an important step for Vance. In *Hillbilly Elegy*, Vance talks at some length about his almost obsessive desire to clerk for a prestigious federal judge, possibly with the goal of becoming a clerk for a US Supreme Court justice. Yet, Vance admits that this was an ambition that he seems to have caught from the Yale environment, a desire for a prestigious position that he didn't really understand and that likely didn't conform to his personal goals. After wise counsel from mentors, particularly Professor Amy Chua, Vance clerked for a federal trial court judge—a less prestigious position but one that afforded an excellent opportunity to observe trials and get practical, on-the-ground experience of how the federal trial court system works.

After his clerkship, Vance spent about two years in corporate law at Sidley Austin, a global law firm based in Chicago—the same firm where Barack and Michelle Obama once worked. Many young attorneys who go into big law firms burn out for the simple reason that they work extremely long hours in an incredibly competitive and stressful environment. But it is likely that there was more than typical big-law burnout to explain Vance's quick departure from legal practice. In *Hillbilly Elegy*, Vance admits that he only went to law school because he didn't know about many careers for successful people other than law and he wanted to be a successful person. Vance clearly wanted to be successful, but it was never clear that he actually wanted to practice law. So in 2016, three years after graduating from Yale Law School (and right around the time that *Hillbilly Elegy* was published), he left the practice of law and began working in venture capital.

From 2016 to 2017, he went to Silicon Valley and worked with Peter Thiel at Mithril Capital, a venture capital firm. This was a pivotal moment for his career path. While Yale Law opened doors to an elite legal and professional world that Vance had never dreamed of, Silicon Valley was a different network altogether. Here, Vance was exposed to and befriended some of the most wealthy and innovative economic leaders in the nation. And in particular, the friendship Vance developed with Thiel would eventually lead to a donation of at least $10 million by Thiel to a super PAC that backed Vance early on in his primary campaign for the US Senate. Without this connection to Thiel, it is unlikely he would have had the funding to win the competitive primary and launch his political career.

As Vance explains in an essay that will be covered later on, he felt drawn back to his home state and did not want to raise a family among the elite class of Silicon Valley that he had become a part of. So despite his developing career in venture capital in Silicon Valley, the heart of the tech and venture capital economy, he decided to move back to Ohio. In 2017, he met Steve Case, co-founder of AOL, who was working in venture capital with a focus on bringing investment capital to underserved areas in the United States. Vance found his way to return home, to focus on his home state, and try to bring resources to communities like the one he grew up in. Vance joined Case's firm, Revolution, and spent about two years there. This brought Vance back to Ohio, where he resided from 2017 until the vice presidency relocated him to Washington, DC.

In 2019, after over three years learning the world of venture capital, Vance co-founded Narya Capital, a venture capital firm based in Cincinnati, Ohio. Big names in venture capital, including Peter Thiel and Marc Andreessen, were backers of the endeavor. By this point, Vance had clearly developed the network—a crucial skill he learned at Yale—to rise into the elite. Thiel, Case, and Andreessen were among the wealthiest and most successful venture capitalists in the nation. He befriended them and convinced them to support his new endeavor. Vance worked at Narya until he began his political campaign for the Senate. With the combined success of *Hillbilly Elegy* and several years in venture capital, Vance accumulated the wealth and connections to run for office. He earned millions while he made friends among the most successful businessmen and most influential conservative minds in the country. From the US Marines to Yale Law to Silicon Valley, every step of Vance's career gave him the skills and connections that would serve him well as he ascended to high political office.

During these years, Vance also became more involved in political endeavors. He served on the boards of American Moment (a conservative, DC-based organization that helps train and place young Conservatives in government staff positions in Washington, DC) and With Honor (a political action committee that helped support military veterans running for political office). The connections he made in the years 2016–2021, both in venture capital and in politics, helped build the base of supporters that would launch his campaign for the US Senate.

This biographical background of Vance is crucial to understanding his political thought and his priorities as a leader in the new Republican Party. Vance comes from the demographic that is now the core of the Republican Party: ordinary, middle American working-class people who feel ignored and left behind by the nation's elites. While Vance has become part of that governing elite, he brings a background, a story, and a perspective that give him a unique love for ordinary American workers and families that is crucial to reshaping Republican politics in America.

III

Insights from *Hillbilly Elegy*

Vance's memoir and social commentary, *Hillbilly Elegy*,[3] turned him from an unknown American success story to a man with a national public image. The brilliance of the book is that it is both a personal autobiography—telling us much about Vance's life and formative experiences—and a powerful commentary on the greatest social problems plaguing the working class. So, while the previous chapter summarized JD Vance's biography, it is also worth exploring some of the cultural and political insights found in *Hillbilly Elegy*. As Vance wrote about his family, community, education, and achievement of the American dream, he laid out some of his deepest and most consistent convictions about social problems, politics, and culture. The themes found in *Hillbilly Elegy* are further developed and remain constant

---

[3] JD Vance, *Hillbilly Elegy* (William Collins, 2016).

through Vance's political writings, speeches, and thought in the years following the publication of the book. But Vance's public intellectual life starts here and so we should too.

What It Takes to Achieve the American Dream Is Not Simply Wealth or Intelligence

This book returns constantly to Vance's understanding of the American dream, not as the acquisition of wealth and material success, but the achievement of a stable family life where one can be a good spouse and a good parent supporting his family with meaningful work. Vance clearly developed this understanding of the American dream through the experience of his own family. In the early chapters of *Hillbilly Elegy*, Vance discusses his grandparents' move from Kentucky to Ohio, seeking better wages and a better life. In a way, they achieved it. Their outward life "was quite successful: My grandfather earned a wage that was almost unfathomable to friends back home; he liked his work and did it well; their children went to modern, well-funded schools; and my grandmother lived in a home that was, by Jackson [KY] standards, a mansion—two thousand square feet, four bedrooms, and modern plumbing." Mamaw and Papaw achieved an outward version of the American dream, acquiring a wage, a home, and a standard of living far beyond what they grew up with.

But "[h]ome life was different." They may have had the exterior trappings of a quiet, stable suburban life, but Vance's grandparents brought their problems with them to their new home. The fights were loud and chaotic, sometimes almost deadly. Papaw's brothers would visit and they would "go out drinking and chasing women." Vance's reflection on these two different lives of his grandparents—the impression given to outsiders and the internal reality—greatly affected him and still affects his view of what it means to succeed. Yes, his grandparents got out of poor Jackson, Kentucky. But they brought much of their inherited violence, dysfunction, and chaos with them. Vance's mother grew up in suburban Ohio but carried on many of the same destructive behaviors. For Vance, then, it is clear that the American dream he was able to achieve (and the American dream that he wants to be available to all Americans) is not about material improvement but about meaningful work and stable family life.

From this perspective, it makes sense that Vance truly believes he "didn't write this book because I've accomplished something extraordinary. I wrote this book because I've achieved something quite ordinary." Vance did not intend, at least not primarily, to write a memoir about his journey from a working-class hillbilly community to Yale Law School and Silicon Valley. That part of the story is in fact extraordinary. But his greatest achievement that he wanted to highlight by writing the book was ordinary, or at least it should be: he became the husband to a loving wife, is raising kids in a good, stable home, does meaningful work that supports his family, and his wife and children do not experience the violence, substance abuse, and general chaos that was part of the family life he experienced as a child. This is his great achievement.

Vance is very quick to point out that his achievements, both familial stability and professional successes, are not due to his own hard work nor to luck. "Today people look at me, at my job and my Ivy League credentials, and assume that I'm some sort of genius, that only a truly extraordinary person could have made it to where I am today. With all due respect to those people, I think that theory is a load of bullshit. Whatever talents I have, I almost squandered until a handful of loving people rescued me."

This is not the success story of an individual, but of a community. Vance would not have had the quiet, stability, and peace to get his grades up and study in high school if Mamaw had not taken him in. Her sacrifice of providing for him, despite her old age and poverty, and sharing her meager resources with her grandson gave JD a chance. His sister Lindsay cared for him for his entire life, showing him (in many ways) the unconditional love of a mother, then later the example of someone who rises above dysfunctional relationships, marries a good man, and has happy, healthy children. His mother's sister, Aunt Wee, married a good, Catholic man and showed JD while he was still a kid that people like them could have healthy marriages.

After Vance left Middletown, professors at Yale, especially Amy Chua, introduced Vance into the inside world of elite law and professional networking. Professor Chua helped guide Vance to see what he really wanted to do with his career after Yale. Her mentorship helped Vance actually understand the inside of the world he was entering, a place that was quite foreign to him. She explained to him the realities of the types of jobs everyone talked about at Yale (what *is* an appellate clerkship? What is "big law" really like?) as well as what it takes to acquire such jobs.

Professor Chua also encouraged him in his relationship with one of the most important "loving people" that rescued him, his wife Usha. Despite their polar opposite upbringings, Usha handled Vance's baggage with a beautiful love and patience. When his learned bad habits took over and he exploded with anger or refused to deal with his emotions during an argument, Usha did not leave. She stayed with him, helped him to grow and work through his troubles. Vance calls Usha his "spirit guide" throughout his time at Yale. Her consistent love helped him to be transformed from an angry kid, who was in many ways a product of his environment, into the husband and father he dreamed of being.

Vance's explanation of why he was able to rise above his circumstances and achieve the American dream is not just a personal story. It offers an insight into how he views the problems that plague the new Republican base—working-class Americans. Vance knows that systemic issues have gutted local communities and left them with a sense of hopelessness due to a lack of meaningful work, stable families, and thriving neighborhoods and towns. He also knows that these circumstances have left many people inclined to make very bad choices.

But Vance is ultimately convinced that government solutions or admonishments to make good personal choices are not a sufficient answer to what ails us. People cannot rise up to overcome what they do not see. They need help. In order to rebuild cultures and save working-class people from despair, people need others who can help. They need family and friends who will lend a hand, set an example, and show the members of their communities a better way. Politics and government policy have an important role to play. But that role is not to solve all societal problems, but to create better conditions for more people to have stable families and stable work, so they can improve their own situations and then lead the way so others can do the same. This is at the heart of what Vance wants to accomplish in public life: "I am acutely aware of how fortunate I am, and even more convinced that we must extend the sort of luck I've had to more children—no matter how difficult. That, to me, is the critical question...."

America's Problem Is Primarily One of Class and Culture, Not Race

While Vance does not focus on race in *Hillbilly Elegy*, the commentary he does offer is profound. Early on in the book, he remarks that there

> is an ethnic component lurking in the background of my story. In our race-conscious society, our vocabulary often extends no further than the color of someone's skin—'black people,' 'Asians,' 'white privilege.' Sometimes these broad categories are useful, but to understand my story, you have to delve into the details. I may be white, but I do not identify with the WASPs of the Northeast. Instead, I identify with the millions of working class white Americans of Scots-Irish descent who have no college degree. To these folks, poverty is the family tradition—their ancestors were day laborers in the Southern slave economy, sharecroppers after that, coal miners after that, and machinists and millworkers during more recent times. Americans call them hillbillies, rednecks, or white trash. I call them neighbors, friends, and family.

The few thoughts about race, class, and hillbilly culture found in *Hillbilly Elegy* are not central to the thesis of the book. But as race-based issues have returned to dominate the national conversation for over a decade now, Vance's insights on race and class are important to the continued national dialogue on the issue.

JD VANCE AND THE FUTURE OF THE REPUBLICAN PARTY

There is much talk about "white privilege" in modern discourse. Historically, certain skin colors would expose one to disadvantage and discrimination. So merely having the appearance of light skin has had its advantages in America, especially for European immigrants in their efforts to assimilate into American life. That being said, there has been a dangerous effort in recent years to make everything about race, to claim that to "be white" is to be part of the superior class in America and that to be a "person of color" is to be perpetually disadvantaged in every area of life. This is not hyperbole. Listen to DEI (diversity, equity, and inclusion) "experts" (or just watch Matt Walsh's "Am I Racist?") and it is clear that there is a real movement to convince people that there is a bright line in American society; "white" people are privileged and "people of color" are not.

This manufactured race crisis in modern America is severely undermined by Vance's observation about his hillbilly people. "Ostensibly, [hillbillies] were of the same racial order (whites) as those who dominated economic, political, and social power in local and national arenas. But *hillbillies* shared many regional characteristics with the southern blacks arriving in Detroit." The reason this is so powerful (and the reason I put "white" in quotation marks above) is because it is horribly overbroad and inaccurate to refer to "white people" in America at all.

The elite class of American government and society has, for most of US history, been "white." But "white" does not simply mean anyone with fair skin. Nearly all of our founders, as well as almost all the presidents of the first 150 years of US history, were Protestants of English descent (Andrew Jackson was the son of Scots Irish immigrants). This "white" culture meant something very specific. It meant men of English ancestry, most of whom belonged to certain mainline Protestant denominations. Irish,

German, Italian, and eastern European immigrants to America looked "white" but were discriminated against and were not treated as part of a privileged class. The discrimination did not occur because their skin was a different color, but because they were cultural outsiders. To put it simply, "white" is an artificial classification that says nothing about a person's culture, upbringing, or way of life. While English descendants of Mayflower pilgrims, Italian immigrants to New York, Pennsylvania Dutch farmers of German descent, and the Ukrainian communities in the Northeast may all appear to be "white," there is no common race among them.

Vance does not make this point at length, nor is race a major point of his book. But he makes a powerful statement when he simply points out that his Scots Irish hillbilly family and community has very little in common with the white English inhabitants of the northeastern United States. When his grandparents (and many other Appalachian hillbillies) moved from Kentucky and West Virginia to places like Middletown, Ohio, the local residents were in a state of culture shock. As Vance points out, his people (though "white" in skin color) had much more in common culturally with the southern black migrants to these same areas than they did with the local "white" residents.

The point is not to dwell on race, but simply to make the observation that Scots Irish hillbillies are "white" yet seem to have basically no advantage as a result of their light skin color. "[I]t is in Greater Appalachia where the fortunes of working-class whites seem dimmest. From low social mobility to poverty to divorce and drug addiction, my home is a hub of misery." Vance's comments point out a hard truth. Many of the problems that are often attributed to race and racism today (poverty, lack of access to good schools, substance abuse, family instability, and so on) were very much present in his "white" community. Vance highlights this simply to show "how class and family affect the poor without filtering their views through a racial prism." Blaming these problems on race doesn't make much sense when they clearly affect poor and working-class Americans of every skin color.

The Fallout of a Deindustrialized America

Systemic circumstances alone cannot be blamed for the poverty and dysfunction of Vance's hillbilly people; he is very clear about this. He tells a story in the introduction of *Hillbilly Elegy* of a young man, only nineteen years old with a pregnant girlfriend, who was given a well-paying job at a tile warehouse. He regularly missed work, showed up late, and took (absurdly) extended bathroom breaks. His pregnant girlfriend was also given a job answering the phone, but she missed work constantly and only lasted a few months. The boyfriend too was fired. The fired employee's response was outrage and complete inability to accept any personal responsibility for his terrible work habits: "How could you do this to me? Don't you know I've got a pregnant girlfriend?"

Vance turns to anecdotes like this often to respond to the idea that people are poor and disadvantaged due to "lack of opportunity" or "the system." Many social commentators point to a lack of good jobs and meaningful opportunities in the lives of lower-class people. But this young man had a good job and an opportunity to work hard and save money to support his girlfriend and new baby. He didn't work hard; he barely showed up at all. Then he blamed others for a situation he caused. Vance points out that this kind of thing happened frequently in Middletown. Despite good wages being paid by this employer, several employees left while Vance was there and the "managers found it impossible to fill my warehouse position with a long-term employee." Sometimes the narrative that poor and unemployed people are mostly good, hard-working folks who simply don't have job prospects doesn't conform to reality. Sometimes there are indeed opportunities, but people fail to take them and to improve their circumstances.

Vance does not simply blame these people for making the bad choice; he contextualizes many of these bad situations as more than just poor choices by free people. There are various serious issues in his community: "Too many young men immune to hard work. Good jobs impossible to fill for any length of time.... There is a lack of agency here—a feeling that you have little control over your life and a willingness to blame everyone but yourself." These people are not solely to blame for their own bad choices. There is a societal problem leading them to feel and act this way.

This feeling of hopelessness, that one has no control and that no decision matters, leads to terrible decisions. But that feeling, wrong as it is, does not come from nowhere and it is not easy to correct. One can hardly blame people for feeling that life is unstable and unfair, given what has happened in these once thriving manufacturing hubs. This is a theme of Vance's book and his thought: "what goes on in the lives of real people when the industrial economy goes south. It's about reacting to bad circumstances in the worst way possible. It's about a culture that increasingly encourages social decay instead of counteracting it."

This book will return to the theme of recovering America's manufacturing base as a central priority of Vance's politics. But for now, it is worth highlighting the reason Vance cares so deeply about this issue. American industry is about more than stable jobs; it is about stable *communities*. When towns and counties are built around a major manufacturing plant, jobs are stable and wages are high. But so much more is going on as a result of that economic situation than individual wages. The company invests in the community and its schools, parks, and sports teams. The people in the community take pride in building a useful product for their community and their country. And perhaps most importantly, people have a sense of hope that their neighbors and friends, their children and grandchildren, will be able to continue to do well in this community because of the presence of a stable community employer. Armco, a steel manufacturer, provided that stability and pride to Middletown, Ohio for decades and gave thousands of people a better life. When that work began to dry up and disappear, the whole community spiraled downward. Thus, the reshoring of manufacturing jobs to the United States is not merely a priority to provide good jobs to Americans; it is an important way to rebuild stable, hopeful American towns and communities.

Conservative Politics Moving Forward

This book is not just about Vance, but about his place in the development and the identity of the Republican Party after President Trump leaves office. Therefore, later chapters will devote much time to Vance's vision of the future of the Republican Party and conservative politics generally. But as Vance concludes *Hillbilly Elegy*, after reflecting on the problems of his life, his family, his community, and the nation, he begins to touch on the biggest political problems of our time. And he wonders "whether our politics are remotely up to the challenge."

It is well known that Vance in particular and the "New Right" movement within the Republican Party are willing to challenge Republican orthodoxies of the past few decades—from free markets to free trade to involvement in foreign wars. Vance signaled early on in his public life that he was open to such breaks from orthodoxy, and indeed that he thinks they are necessary: "my own party has to abandon the dogmas of the 1990s and actually offer something of substance to working- and middle-class Americans." To be fair, this is not simply a criticism of the Republican Party as misguided. Vance's criticism is more that the party continues to try applying the same remedies as it did in decades past, even though the diseases of the day are different and require different treatment. The problem is not simply government overregulation or incorrect policy, but rather severe cultural decay that goes beyond what government can remedy. The Republican Party needs to adjust and realign accordingly. Perhaps this realignment is now obvious, but Vance knew it had to happen nearly a decade ago, before it was mainstream. The Republican Party has moved from being the party of big business and the wealthy elite to the party of the working class. It has to accept that identity, then campaign and govern accordingly.

So what should these policy shifts look like? Vance offers many details about this question in later writings, but was still figuring it out when he wrote *Hillbilly Elegy*. While the book is light on specific policy proposals—it is a memoir, after all—he does diagnose some of the problems that the Republican platform failed to address for years. He points to Donald Trump's valid criticism of American "foreign policy blunders in Iraq and Afghanistan." On the domestic front, he addresses the core social problems that Republicans need to take more seriously, particularly the epidemic of drug overdoses and rising mortality rates. And he highlights an economic shift that is finally gaining momentum within the conservative movement today: "Despite a relatively vibrant economy, many of the regional economies in the industrial Midwest continue to struggle, wage growth lags behind productivity growth...." In this quotation Vance highlights a serious issue that we will cover later on: the growth of the macro economy, the rise of the stock market or the Gross Domestic Product (GDP), and does not necessarily reflect the economic health of average Americans.

These three issues mentioned at the end of *Hillbilly Elegy*—rethinking foreign policy, addressing deadly social issues plaguing America, and reorienting the way Republicans think about economic success—reveal the places where Vance and the "New Right" within the Republican Party have begun to break ranks with the "dogmas of the 1990s" that Vance warns about. These changes have moved from the peripheries to the mainstream within Republican politics. When Vance wrote these words, he worried that not enough Conservatives within the movement were likely to accept and embrace the changes to the party platform that were desperately needed in our day: "For so many years, I and a few of my intellectual fellow travelers in the Republican Party were telling politicians to make precisely these sorts of [populist] arguments." Vance realized that without these changes and priorities that the working-class cares deeply about, the Republican Party would be in deep trouble. And it must be clear that *campaigning* on a new platform is not enough; the party needs to appoint the right people and adopt the correct policy priorities when *governing*, not simply when enticing voters during election season. Vance worried around 2016 that the "populist rhetoric of the [Trump] campaign hasn't informed the party's approach to governing. Unless that changes, I suspect Republicans will pay a heavy political price."

It seems Vance was correct in his diagnosis. There are real changes being made within the Republican Party. Not too many years ago, intervention in foreign conflicts in the name of spreading democracy or toppling dictatorships was quite acceptable among the largely neoconservative Republicans. Today, prominent Republican leaders (Vance a strong voice among them during his time in the Senate) have voiced opposition to continued foreign wars. Avoiding wars that do not directly affect the national interest is becoming more and more mainstream in Republican politics. President Trump himself, in his inaugural address on January 20, 2025, highlighted the goodness of such an approach to military involvement: "We will measure our success not only by the battles we win, but also by the wars that we end, and perhaps most importantly, the wars we never get into."

On economics, the Republican Party has long been wed to free markets, GDP growth, and the ideal of government nonintervention in economics as almost religious dogmas. This is also shifting. Vance's concern in the afterword of *Hillbilly Elegy* about wage growth lagging behind productivity growth was prescient. Conservative intellectuals like Oren Cass at American Compass have done an excellent job writing about this issue. When corporate profits and GDP grow but the wages of workers stagnate, we have a problem. The Republicans are now the party of the working class and the working class wants a good living wage, not a good quarterly report on GDP. There is also a real societal problem. If the American economy continues to grow, the stock market goes up, corporate profit reports look great, but the wages of the working man (who makes up a supermajority of the nation's population) are not going up, we are putting the wrong emphasis on how we measure economic success as a society. Vance highlighted this years ago and the Republican Party, now realigning around the needs of American workers, is catching on.

Vance's focus on workers, healthy families and communities, and a more sane and restrained foreign policy has been part of his political thought for nearly a decade. This focus is becoming more prominent within the Republican Party as a whole, as the party adapts to new twenty-first century problems and a new working-class coalition. It is a great asset to the Republican Party and to the nation that one of the great intellectual leaders of this political realignment, a man who has been thinking through and writing about these pressing issues for years before they became mainstream conversations, is now the vice president of the United States and most likely the leader of the post-Trump GOP.

A Man Like Us

The final major takeaway from Vance's *Hillbilly Elegy* for those interested in the future of American politics is simply this: Vance is uniquely brilliant and extremely talented, but his background and experiences reveal that he is a normal guy. He is more or less like us. This is relevant because politics is about telling voters a story. And unlike many politicians, Vance's story is actually interesting and relatable.

Vance came from a broken home in middle America. He came from poverty, marital strife, and dysfunction. He came close to failing out of school. He overcame tremendous odds, thanks to a couple key people in his extended family and community who took an interest in him. And his hard work, coupled with fortunate encounters with a few of the right people, led him out of the hopelessness of his surroundings and into the Marine Corps, Ohio State, Yale Law School, Silicon Valley, the US Senate, and the vice presidency.

The story of JD Vance is a real rags-to-riches story; there is no need for communications experts to spin Vance's life and make it seem interesting or relatable. Vance's life story is the American dream and that should give hope to many Americans. When we look at JD Vance, we do not see a trust-fund kid. We do not see a political success whose father was also a political success. We see someone with no privilege and no advantage. We see someone whose natural abilities, hard work, and providential encounters with the right people at the right time led him from hillbilly dysfunction to a loving family life, as well as to the highest ranks of American society. In an age where fewer and fewer people believe that their children will do better than they have done, a story like Vance's is a source of hope.

Politics is pragmatic. At the end of the day, voters should want to elect people who will enact good policies for the good of the nation. We are not primarily voting for role models or those whose personal lives serve as examples to us and our children. We vote for those who will do what we need them to do in their office. But ideally, we would have both. So as the rest of this book lays out the intellectual and political reasons that Vance is good for the Republican Party and the nation, it is good to stop and remember that in JD Vance we have a unique figure who is both statesman and personal role model. Yes, Vance is a talented conservative intellectual, possibly the best hope of the Republican Party to balance successful policy with political victory. But in Vance, we also get the unique figure of a man who has overcome poverty and dysfunction. We get a man who is sincere, devout, and religious. We get a leader who loves and cares deeply for his wife and children. In summary, Vance stands as that classical ideal. He is the statesman who we can hold up as both a political leader and a personal role model for those he serves.

IV

Vance's Early Political Writings

There are several interesting essays Vance wrote in the years around the release of *Hillbilly Elegy*. Two of these early essays are particularly helpful in understanding the thought and the political life of JD Vance. The first reveals Vance's candid look at Barack Obama, a politician he disagreed with on practically everything but in whom he still found something to admire. The second talks about Vance's love of his home state and why he left Silicon Valley to return to Ohio. Both essays say a lot about Vance's character and what he prioritizes and loves.

JD Vance: Obama Fan?

Vance wrote a short op-ed in the New York Times in 2017 titled *Barack Obama and Me*.[4] The existence of this essay is fascinating because it is so obviously candid. The piece was published in the immediate aftermath of *Hillbilly Elegy* becoming a bestseller and JD Vance becoming a nationally known public figure. At this point, Donald Trump was already president and had taken his place as leader of the Republican Party. And Vance was already a prominent conservative name. It is unlikely that a Republican in 2017 with explicit political ambitions to run for elected office would have written an op-ed showing any kind of admiration for Barack Obama. So it seems fairly likely that Vance was reflecting on politics and culture candidly in this essay, without political ambitions.

The op-ed begins with Vance explaining his first introduction to politics as a child during the Bill Clinton era. Vance admired Clinton as "one of us," a poor boy with an accent, raised by a single mother and involved grandparents. Vance loved that Clinton had "made it," not by becoming wealthy and successful, but by (apparently) leaving behind the poverty and family dysfunction of his young life in Arkansas and achieving the domestic tranquility that he lacked in his own upbringing. The Clinton sex scandal destroyed that vision of Clinton, but at the time it made an impression on young Vance to see someone who grew up in a situation like his rise above his circumstances.

This essay gave another instance of a powerful common theme in Vance's writings: even as a boy watching some of the most famous and powerful men on the planet, it was not their wealth

---

[4] JD Vance, "Barack Obama and Me," *NY Times*, January 2, 2017, https://www.nytimes.com/2017/01/02/opinion/barack-obama-and-me.html.

or professional success that made the impression that they had "made it." What Vance was looking for as a model of success, even in politicians, was people who had risen from poverty and dysfunction to achieve good jobs and happy families.

When Obama came on the scene, Vance, scarred by the betrayal of the Clinton scandal, assumed some dark scandal must also lie beneath the surface of Obama's life. Surely this appearance of overcoming a tough background to achieve success and domestic tranquility must be a mask. Surely people like them don't actually "make it"—Clinton taught him that. But Vance reflects on the Obama presidency and maintains that Obama really did come out of it. Obama barely knew his father, did not have a stable home, and got involved in drugs as a teenager. Despite the family dysfunction, Vance observed that Obama and his wife appear to love and respect each other, love their children, and have no serious issues of addiction, violence, and so on. This simple example offered Vance hope of escaping an unstable childhood experience and achieving a happy marriage with thriving children. Vance seems to have carried around a sad assumption for most of his young life, an assumption that a life of domestic tranquility (free of violence, shouting, abuse, substance use, and general dysfunction) was only for those who came from normal, intact families. His belief for many years was that such a happy, stable life was unavailable to people like him. Obama was the first major political figure who caught Vance's attention as an example of rising above his circumstances. Obama was someone whose life showed that a broken childhood did not make the cycle inevitable.

Again, remembering that it is unlikely Vance was writing this piece for political expediency (a conservative Republican in 2016 had little to gain by saying anything positive about Barack

Obama), there are a couple candid points to be gleaned from this op-ed. Vance argues that polarized politics often prevents Conservatives from making an important distinction. We might disagree with Barack Obama on every area of policy (Vance does), but Vance still maintains that Obama "himself is an admirable man." Politics aside, Obama had some personal merit. His life gave Vance "hope that a boy who grew up like me could still achieve the most important of my dreams."

Stepping back from Barack Obama in particular, there is a general point that Conservatives would do well to reflect on here. It is important not to turn politics into an all-consuming, tribal affair. Yes, Conservatives have serious disagreements with Liberals about almost everything. These are not mere trivial disagreements on unimportant areas of policy; sometimes the disagreements are about the very way we view the world, what is good, and what is evil. The differences matter greatly. But there is a danger that politics can turn our minds to consider all political rivals as absolute villainous people, rotten to the core, in whom no good whatsoever can be found. Vance rightly cautions us to avoid that. We will have a much saner political and social life if, while fighting hard and pulling no punches in our political discourse, we respect our political opponents as *people* rather than treating them like demons.

This change of perspective Vance advocates has two related benefits. On a personal level, it is important for Conservatives to be good, decent, virtuous people. To be clear, this *does not* mean adopting a false political civility where we fail to confront evil and to boldly call out bad ideas. It means maintaining a remembrance of the humanity of the people with whom we fight. Yes, our political opponents might be wrong on every issue. They might advocate a worldview that is downright toxic. So, fight them we must. But many of them are good, decent people with very bad ideas. Even the ones who seem to be personally bad people, we (especially Christians) must remember that each of these people is made in the image and likeness of God.

Politics is extremely important, but it is not everything. A baseline level of humanity and respect should be maintained for our government leaders, even those we disagree with most. And by maintaining that view, we may be able to find some redeemable ideas or qualities within them. That does not mean we ever need to agree with them when they are wrong or appease them in the name of civility. But it does mean we should not hate them. This shift in worldview might help to turn down the temperature of political discourse, even as the disagreements remain intense and the fights continue to be fought.

Perhaps surprisingly, this shift in perspective has a political benefit. If we view our political opponents as humans, not simply as the enemy, it becomes possible to build coalitions and make political compromises. In our current political climate, many Conservatives see people on the Left as America-hating, Marxist, woke enemies who want to destroy the country and everything we love. Given the political platform of many Democrats in recent years, such an extreme reaction is understandable. But the reality is about half of our nation's elected officials are Democrats. Congress is governed by extremely narrow majorities. Many state governments are split between a legislature of one party and a governor of another party. In such a divided political climate, it is impossible to accomplish much of anything if you view the other side as an enemy to be destroyed. Sometimes compromise on a certain issue can yield results for the common good—even if not the pure, perfect result that would be possible if compromise were not needed. All people who are serious about politics and policy know that trade-offs are sometimes necessary. Tempering our view of the other side as consisting of people, not demons, makes for more rational and effective conservative leaders.

So perhaps most supporters of JD Vance shudder at his 2016 op-ed praising Barack Obama. And given Vance's evolution in recent years (as the next two chapters will discuss, Vance has grown to think of the political establishment and America's institutions as much more corrupt than he once thought), perhaps he wouldn't be so quick to praise anything about Barack Obama today. But the lesson in the op-ed remains valid: if we can learn to see our opponents as people—even wrong and extremely misguided people—rather than pure enemies to be destroyed, perhaps we can find the ability to work with them when possible, or at least not hate them while we fight them.

Vance Goes Home to Ohio

Another early and candid written work from Vance was a 2017 op-ed in the *New York Times* titled *Why I'm Moving Home*.[5] Before moving into the main topic of the essay—Vance's decision to return home to Ohio—he makes a point about the cultural effects of "brain drain" and hyper-polarization that is worthy of mention.

"Brain drain," the phenomenon where the most talented and intelligent young people from small towns tend to move to big metropolitan cities in search of better social and economic prospects, has more than an economic effect on society. Vance cites a study from the RAND Corporation arguing that brain drain

---

[5] J.D. Vance, "Why I'm Moving Home," *NY Times,* March 16, 2017, https://www.nytimes.com/2017/03/16/opinion/why-im-moving-home.html.

has actually deepened America's political polarization in recent decades. How does this work? Vance explains his experience of the trend with an anecdote:

> Not long before the election, a friend forwarded me a conspiracy theory about Bill and Hillary Clinton's involvement in a pedophilia ring and asked me whether it was true. It's easy to dismiss these questions as the ramblings of "fake news" consumers. But the more difficult truth is that people naturally trust the people they know—their friend sharing a story on Facebook—more than strangers who work for faraway institutions. And when we're surrounded by polarized, ideologically homogeneous crowds, whether online or off, it becomes easier to believe bizarre things about [the political elite].

This anecdote speaks volumes about the state of American political life. The "brain drain" phenomenon encourages the "best and brightest" from small towns not to return home after college, but to go and obtain elite jobs and credentials in big coastal cities. So, the well-educated "elite" tend to settle disproportionately in large, liberal cosmopolitan areas, while those who lack formal education and work blue-collar jobs are left in the small towns of America.

The problem is apparent: when one's community does not contain people with diverse levels of education and worldview, biases are re-enforced. This means that ordinary folks in small towns maintain suspicious and sometimes conspiratorial attitudes about the well-educated "elites," because they likely don't know any of them personally. But the "problem runs in both directions: I've heard ugly words uttered about 'flyover country' and some of its inhabitants from well-educated, generally well-meaning people." When people of different political persuasions, levels of education, and life experience are more and more geographically segregated, the polarized partisan divide widens. So ordinary Americans distrust the elites and the elites despise ordinary Americans, because they do not live together and therefore do not know or trust each other.

This reflection on geographical segregation and political polarization is part of what led JD Vance to leave his life and work in Silicon Valley and return to Ohio. Vance notes that the temptations that lead to "brain drain" appealed to him personally. He felt the conflict as a young man. People in regions hit hard by job loss experience a deep tension between the love of their home and the desire to leave in search of better economic opportunities. Vance loved Ohio, but the economic opportunities available to him after school were simply better elsewhere. While experts encourage mobility so that people from depressed areas (people like Vance himself) can move to places with greater job opportunities and lower unemployment. This has problematic consequences for small-town communities. When the best and brightest regularly leave their local communities for better opportunities, small towns and entire geographic regions lose their most talented citizens.

This "brain drain" encourages people to detach from their homes and cultures. Those most able to help their local communities instead choose to leave, marry, and settle in economically segregated cities and communities. The wealthy, bright, upper-class folks all live in the same places, which means many American communities have lost their brightest citizens, those who should be the natural leaders of those communities. More people (like Vance) need to consciously make the decision that it is ultimately better for individuals, families, and communities if talented people try to remain in the communities from which they come and to make those communities a better place. More people should stay home and make their home a better place. This is not only better for the community; it is ultimately better for the happiness of the individual as well. Wouldn't most smart young people be happier surrounded by the family and friends they grew up with, starting companies, running for office, and succeeding in their hometown than becoming an overworked cog in the machine of a major corporation or consulting firm in Boston or New York?

Besides the loss of leadership, this geographic segregation allows members of both sides of the political aisle to live in increasingly polarized echo chambers. Members of the elite become increasingly smug and convinced that they are right, while working-class Americans become more and more prone to a politics of bitterness and conspiracy theories. What is the answer to this segregated polarization? Quite frankly, there is no easy answer or policy solution. There needs to be a culture shift. Cultural leaders like Vance leading the way and explaining their decision is an important start.

After two years in Silicon Valley, surrounded by the elites and their great lives, Vance was sobered by how optimistic his peers were about life and the future, while most of the people he grew up around were full of pessimism. He lived in a world of personal, professional, and economic success, where "every person feels his life will only get better." While this has its benefits—it is easier to succeed and be optimistic when surrounded by successful and optimistic people—something bothered him about the people he was surrounded by. How can you be comfortable around such unqualified success and optimism "when you [come] from a world where many rightfully believe that things have become worse"? Vance suspected that this disconnect caused a real problem of naivete among the elite: "this optimism blinds many in Silicon Valley to the real struggles in other parts of the country." Rather than deal with these Silicon Valley tensions, Vance "decided to move home, to Ohio."

The transition from Silicon Valley back to Ohio involved drastic changes concerning everything from job prospects to quality of school districts to weather. The transition was not easy, but it was important for Vance to go home. What "communities need most is not just financial support, but talent and energy and committed citizens to build viable businesses and other civic institutions." Vance's statement here is an important one, but more important is that he acted on it. It is one thing to make the sociological observation that more people should take their elite credentials back to their hometowns rather than take fancy jobs in major cities. It is quite another thing to actually act on it, leave an amazing job in Silicon Valley, and return to Ohio to try to help one's own community and people. If more people finished their degrees and took their talents back to their communities rather than fleeing to big law firms and cushy consulting gigs in New York, Boston, DC, and San Francisco, such a change could transform the country.

When we ask ourselves where and how we ought to live, Vance's reflection should be a part of the calculation: "whether the choices we make for ourselves are necessarily the best for our home communities—and for the country." Of course, it would not be prudent to choose poverty, an economic dead end where we literally were unable to obtain meaningful work. But the reality is that we live in a technologically advanced age, one where educated white-collar professionals are more and more able to work from anywhere in the country. Perhaps this choice to go back home rather than be another cog in the machine of a big city economy contains the possibility of greater personal fulfillment as well as benefits to a local community. As I asked before, wouldn't many people be more fulfilled as leaders back in their little hometowns—as mayors and business owners, doctors and lawyers, in a place where they can make a real impact—than as high-paid city-dwellers living among countless other professionals stuck in the same rat race? Maybe Vance is on to something. Maybe most of us are better off taking our time and talents back home.

Vance's decision to move back to Ohio says something about his priorities. Vance spent much of his political life—from his first published writings to his first days in the Senate dealing with the horrible train crash in East Palestine, OH—advocating for policies that help ordinary American individuals, families, and communities. He moved back to Ohio in 2017, a full four years before he announced his campaign for the US Senate. The move back to his hometown was clearly an attempt to work for and effect change in his community, not to relocate solely in order to run for political office. Vance's move back to Ohio shows that he walked the walk. He cared enough about his home to leave the elite community to which he gained admission in Silicon Valley so that he could live, work, raise a family, and serve among his own people.

V

Vance and the Poisoned Garden of America

Critics often take aim at Vance's political evolutions. The accusation is that he has changed his views over the years for personal gain. They say he has shifted with the political winds in his stances on particular policy issues, President Trump, and the way he engages in political rhetoric.

Vance certainly has changed, but the best explanation is not political expediency or a lack of principles. The most plausible explanation for the evolution of JD Vance is simply a shift in how he views the state of American institutions. Vance explains where he stands on the state of America—and what is required to fix it—in a short but profound analogy: the poisoned garden. Perhaps the place where Vance best articulates this is in an excellent foreword that he wrote for Dr. Kevin Roberts' book *Dawn's Early Light*.

Kevin Roberts is a particularly important and interesting conservative thinker. He's an historian by trade and a former president of a Catholic liberal arts college. Roberts and JD Vance both share a poor upbringing in an unstable family and an intelligent Conservative politics willing to break with many of the Republican orthodoxies of recent decades. So it was quite natural that, when Roberts wrote a book about what it will take for Conservatives to save America and restore it to greatness, JD Vance was asked to write the foreword to the book.[6]

There is much to be gleaned from this short written work by Vance. First of all, it is significant that Vance agreed to write the foreword at all. Dr. Kevin Roberts is a great intellectual on the modern Right and he leads the Heritage Foundation, one of the largest and most influential conservative organizations in the country. The fact that Vance understands the importance of Heritage, the brilliance of Roberts, and the need for the type of conservative philosophical thinking found in this book says something important about the type of conservative thinker Vance is. JD Vance is a politician and a successful one. But he understands the need to have a bridge and close connection between the conservative intellectuals who are thinking about, researching, and proposing policies, and the politicians and lawmakers who put those policies into practice. Vance himself serves as an important bridge between the conservative intellectual

---

[6] Alex Shephard, "Read J.D. Vance's Violent Foreword to Project 2025 Leader's New Book," *New Republic*, July 30, 2024, https://newrepublic.com/article/184393/jd-vance-violent-foreword-kevin-roberts-project-2025-leader-book?utm_campaign=SF_TNR&utm_source=Twitter&utm_medium=social.

movement—which he understands deeply and participates in actively—and Republican politics.

While Vance's foreword garnered significant media attention. Outlets like the *New Republic* wrote headlines about Vance's "violent foreword" to the book. This accusation of "violence" was based on the last words of Vance's foreword: "We are now all realizing that it's time to circle the wagons and load the muskets. In the fights that lay ahead, these ideas are an essential weapon." Of course, to label this as a call to violence is absurd. "Circle the wagons and load the muskets" is a metaphor, a call to look inward and come together as a movement. The fact that he refers to conservative *ideas* as an essential weapon makes it quite obvious that this is a metaphorical expression and not a call to arms.

The important analogy and hidden gem in this foreword is not the bit about circling the wagons but a brilliant analogy about a garden, a gardener, and how to remedy poisoned soil. Vance articulates here, perhaps better than anywhere else, his justification for a less libertarian, more muscular conservative movement that is willing to use political power for good ends. To explain his view of the state of affairs in America and his justification for many of his changes in perspective on Trump, conservatism, and the Republican Party, he uses the following:

> Imagine a well-maintained garden in a patch of sunlight. It has some imperfections of course, and many weeds. The very thing that makes it attractive for the things we try to cultivate makes it attractive for the things we don't. In an effort to eliminate the bad, a well-meaning gardener treats the garden with a chemical solution. This kills many of the weeds, but it also kills many

of the good things. Undeterred, the gardener keeps adding the solution. Eventually, the soil is inhospitable.

This is a beautiful, clear explanation of why Conservatives—normally inclined to reject government intervention to solve societal problems—may need to embrace a different view of politics and government in the modern era. It is true that in a healthy climate with good soil and sunlight, little action is needed by the gardener to produce good fruit. But once the soil has been poisoned, it is not enough to stop introducing poison, plant seeds, and let nature take its course again. More than non-intervention is necessary; active steps need to be taken to repair the damage.

The garden is American society and the gardener introducing the chemical poisons is modern liberal ideology. Even if you get rid of the gardener and there is no longer anyone adding poison to the garden, the garden does not recover to full health. The soil is toxic. The damage is done. Healthy things will not grow here.

Vance observes that dangerous ideologies have infected the soil of American institutions: the media, universities, corporations, and government agencies have been poisoned for decades. In this situation, it is no longer enough for the government to stop introducing Leftist policy and to let nature (the private sector) take its course. In a healthy society, a restrained government could simply limit its actions and let families, schools, community associations, and businesses contribute to the building up of healthy citizens and communities. Remove the intervening gardener and let the sunlight and the rainwater take their course, right?

But when the soil has been poisoned, rain and sun are not enough. Removing government intervention and letting private institutions act freely will no longer solve the problems. If universities have stopped prioritizing the pursuit of truth and have chosen to become places of left-wing indoctrination, if the media has moved from reporting facts to promoting propaganda, then government neutrality and non-intervention will not reverse those trends.

This is precisely the case Vance is making to justify a more robust conservative politics. "The garden needs not just to stop adding a terrible solution, though it does need that. It needs to be recultivated." When everything is broken, when American jobs have been outsourced, when media indoctrinates children with bad ideas from an increasingly young age, when private corporations have "gone woke" by enacting DEI policies and restrictions on certain kinds of political speech and action, libertarian government is insufficient to restore the country to health. "The old conservative movement argued if you just got government out of the way, natural forces would resolve problems—we are no longer in this situation and must take a different approach."

The analogy of the poisoned garden should be kept in mind whenever one thinks of the political principles of JD Vance. Vance is not simply a reactionary who wants to do away with limited government conservatism and become a right-wing supporter of big government. To the contrary: throughout his writings, Vance articulates a real appreciation for free markets, limited government, and a greater role for local institutions—from families and churches to small businesses and neighborhood associations. Vance is, at heart, generally a small government Conservative who believes most problems are best solved by local institutions rather than big government programs. But he has come to realize that the major institutions in American life are so influenced and corrupted by modern Liberalism that, in our time, shrinking the government is not enough.

However, it is worth noting that part of Vance's thinking diverges from limited-government Libertarianism as a matter of principle, not just as a practical reaction to how bad he thinks America's institutions have become. Vance, like many non-libertarian Conservatives, believes government does exist to promote the common good. Government, when properly ordered, is a good and necessary thing for human beings; it is not a necessary evil. While corrupt government can be extremely dangerous and there are many reasons to prefer a limited government, government in itself is not bad or unworthy of trust. Therefore, government policy can and should accomplish positive goods. This is a real philosophical distinction between Conservatives like Vance and the Libertarians who have had a strong influence on the Republican Party since at least the 1980s.

Despite Vance's non-libertarian conservative principles, many of his political stances have more to do with the current state of the nation than with his views of the ideal form of government. Like many Conservatives, Vance would probably prefer a garden with healthy soil, plenty of sunlight, and a temperate climate, where very little intervention is needed to produce good fruit. A society with less need for government solutions is the ideal. This is true not because government is bad, but because a community full of strong, intact families, thick extended family networks, healthy neighborhoods, schools, churches, and so on, simply does not have as many problems that require government intervention. But when the institutions are failing, Vance is willing to break rank with the "old-guard" and entertain the idea that it may be prudent for more hands-on government policy solutions to restore what has been lost.

With this analogy of the poisoned garden in mind, Vance's foreword singles out two areas where Dr. Kevin Roberts correctly identifies the need for a shift in thinking on the Right: corporations and families.

The critical focus on corporations is important and refreshing to see from conservative leaders like Vance and Roberts. Both men emphasize the need to re-think how the Right views corporate freedom and power. For quite a while now, Republicans have been inclined to view the government as the main enemy of freedom and, as a consequence, have championed a free market that restricts government intervention and that gives relatively free rein to the actions of private corporations. Vance and Roberts point out two issues (one historical and one practical) that deserve consideration.

Historically, perhaps Conservatives need a wake-up call: "the modern financial corporation was almost entirely foreign to the founders of our nation." While Conservatives often appeal to the wisdom of Adam Smith, the founding of the United States as a nation of commerce, and the dangers of government interference with private entities such as business corporations, nothing like Apple or Google really existed at the time of the American founding. Modern corporations are novel in their size and especially in the fact that they are transnational—they are typically owned and operated by citizens of many countries and not exclusively loyal to the United States.

The founders of the United States were not pure adherents of the free market; they had no problem with certain economic regulations, such as banning gambling and the corporate sale of indecent, pornographic content. Perhaps more important, Corporate America differs from Founding Era-business in that corporations today are not quite as "private" and distinct from the government as the false dichotomy between public and private entities suggests. The founders did not anticipate that major tech companies would collude with government agencies to suppress political information just before a presidential election.

Again, the major corporations of the modern day do not resemble anything the US founders would have known. If there was any corollary to the modern corporation at the time of the American founding, it would have been the British East India Company, which Vance points out was "a monstrous hybrid of public and private power that would have made its subjects completely unable to access an American sense of liberty." And that is precisely the point. Corporations can become so large, so dominant, and so intertwined with public works and governments that they no longer behave like the ordinary corporations that most Americans think of when they express desire for a business climate free from government interference.

Normally, a free market means companies are free from government intervention and excessive regulation. This freedom is intended to enable companies to produce goods and services efficiently and to compete for customers by providing the best prices. But with companies the size of Google or Amazon, it is a completely different situation. These organizations often have the platform and power to control and censor speech; they also communicate (and sometimes cooperate) with government agencies. They are so large that they have monopoly power, which is antithetical to the free market because it allows a single company to arbitrarily set industry prices and eliminate competition. These companies have so much money, power, and influence in American society that to err on the side of government non-interference as a matter of political principle will not unleash free-market prosperity. Such a libertarian philosophy risks allowing private corporations to wield tyrannical power to rival that of a tyrannical government.

In addition to the size of some modern mega-corporations, there is also a woke problem. Many corporations in modern America hire not solely on merit but on the basis of minority status. They discriminate against employees or customers that hold pro-life views or vote for Republican candidates. They subject their employees to DEI trainings and policies. And a wide range of products—from children's clothing to children's movies—have been (more or less quietly, depending on the circumstances) peddling pro-LGBT propaganda through their products and services.

A potential danger of laissez-faire capitalism in the modern economy, one that many ordinary citizens may not know, is that it can no longer be taken for granted that corporations are motivated solely by maximizing profit for their shareholders. At least if they were, we could be confident that the best products are being made as efficiently as possible and that efficient profit seeking is the sole motivation of these free, unregulated businesses. But when corporations are increasingly putting left-wing ideologies into their products, services, and employment practices on a regular basis (even when this loses them money, like Bud Light or Disney's Lightyear movie), the situation has changed.

The concern about woke corporate culture goes back to Vance's analogy of the poisoned garden. In a healthy society, where well-adjusted people from good families grow up to work hard, start businesses, and create useful products as efficiently as possible, relatively free markets make sense. Why should the government interfere at all in a system where people get what they need as cheaply and efficiently as possible? But does the equation change when corporations are not American but transnational, shipping jobs overseas where wages are lower? What happens when they are so big that they cut out all competition and so powerful that they collude with government agencies? What does it look like when they are distributing products, services, and messages that are saturated with toxic ideologies? At a certain point, we have to realize that forces of globalism and woke ideology have invaded the free market and poisoned the garden. Simply removing government regulation may not be sufficient.

The other area of American life that Vance focuses on in his foreword for Roberts' book is the family. We will discuss family policy later on, but the analogy of the poisoned garden is also relevant here. Yes, "cultural norms and attitudes matter. We should encourage our kids to get married and have kids. We should teach them that marriage isn't just a contract, but a sacred and lifelong union. We should discourage them from behaviors that threaten the stability of their families." And yes, these are generally *cultural* norms that are passed down from parents to children, from generation to generation. Just as the gardener should cultivate his garden with love and nourish it so that it grows healthy plants, so families and communities should naturally cultivate the next generation with love and care.

But the soil of the institution of the family has also been poisoned. Globalization and free trade have shipped overseas many of the jobs that made it possible for working-class people to support a family on a single income. The culture has taught children to seek careers and riches over marriages, families, and children and also to contracept and cohabitate instead of getting married and having kids. We are many years removed from a healthy society where stable marriages and families are the norm being passed from one generation to the next. The soil has been poisoned. Globalization, offshoring of manufacturing jobs, anti-family policies and messaging, have all seeped into society for decades and created a culture where getting married, having children, and cultivating a stable, healthy family is not encouraged.

Vance does not offer too many policy specifics here but he suggests that we should be open to government policies that foster "material circumstances such that having a family isn't only for the privileged." Again, mere removal of the gardener and his modern Liberalism will not heal the soil. The culture of selfishness, childlessness, and preferring careers to families, will not wash away without an active effort to restore a culture that promotes family formation. In a healthy community, family formation comes naturally; let the sun shine on the garden and the fruits will grow. But when it is no longer the default for young people to grow up, get married, stay married, and raise children, it is worth seriously considering the possibility of using government policy solutions to fix the landscape and make family formation normative again.

In this short foreword, Vance provides a powerful roadmap with which to navigate a new conservative politics for our day. Yes, we generally prefer free markets and a society where families, private institutions, and local communities shape the culture and government stays out of the way. But decades of bad policy have poisoned the very ground in which our society is rooted. Perhaps we need to do more than simply stop adding poison. Perhaps politics and government must take a more active role in restoring health and prosperity than would be necessary in saner times. This is not about a right-wing version of big government statism. Rather, it is a pragmatic view from the modern Right that is less about enthusiastic use of big government and more about recognizing that certain things have become so bad that they will not improve without intentional action.

VI

Vance Comes Around to Trump

Any profile of JD Vance, especially one that takes Vance seriously both as a thought leader for the future of the Republican Party and as a presidential contender, needs to address Vance's changing posture toward President Donald Trump. Vance went from a fierce critic of Trump to a vocal support of Trump to Trump's vice president. Critics of Vance complain that this change was an act of political expediency, a typical move by a shrewd politician who saw which way the wind was blowing in the Republican Party. That criticism is probably fair when leveled against a good number of prominent Republican politicians over the last decade. The number of Republicans who went from staunchly anti-Trump to full-on MAGA is staggering, and many of them did so without ever really acknowledging the reason for the change (or acknowledging that there had been a change at all).

But Vance stands out not because he was previously a "never Trumper" (he was) or because he changed his views on Trump (most Republicans did), but because he has honestly acknowledged the fact and explained in detail the reasons for the change. Vance's explanation for his Trump conversion is coherent, convincing, and deserving of a full hearing. Vance contends that he did not change substantially on policy or political view; what changed was his view of the state of America and of American institutions. This chapter helps explain not only the legitimacy of Vance's biggest political evolution, but also to explain the legitimacy of establishment Conservatives coming around to MAGA.

Vance Against Trump

As a young writer fairly new to the conservative intellectual scene, Vance was still rather optimistic about America: it had swung to the Left, but he maintained hope that American families, institutions, and communities could be nudged back to health and prosperity. If that analysis of America was correct, then the caustic, negative, and seemingly exaggerated political rhetoric of Donald Trump was an unhelpful and divisive trend in American politics. This was Vance's belief when he wrote *Hillbilly Elegy*, where he noted that he understood some of the populist sentiments in the MAGA movement but that he maintained "reservations about Donald Trump." Vance admits he "ended up voting third party."

Around the time *Hillbilly Elegy* came out, Vance wrote several extremely anti-Trump comments. Among them was an essay at the *Atlantic* called "Opioid of the Masses."[7] Here he laid out his views in 2016 about the plight of middle America, the appeal of Trump's populism, and why he believed Trump was not the answer. According to Vance's account, the breakdown of middle American towns in recent years has ultimately been the tragic story of a people attempting to dull their pain. There is economic pain as factories and other traditional employers downsize and move out. Towns decay with beautiful storefronts replaced by pawn shops and payday lenders. Homes and marriages fall apart. Through all of this, the people have the sense that the politicians and the government don't speak for them. The government fights foreign wars and helps big corporations, but it doesn't care much for the ordinary working man. There is a sense that the government helps others get ahead, not them.

Vance opined that Donald Trump, like opioids and heroin, was a crutch that aggrieved, working-class people were turning to in an attempt to dull the pain. Trump's new base, the realigned working-class that had long been the backbone of the Democratic party, comes from these broken middle American communities. In these places, religious faith is down, good jobs are hard to come by, and addiction and overdose are increasing. There is a general (and understandable) sense of meaninglessness and grievance in these communities.

Trump promised ordinary American working people what Vance characterized as easy solutions: MAGA would enact policies to bring back good American jobs; Trump would fix the open border and end the scourge of drugs brought here by the cartels. Vance acknowledged that Trump's campaign identified

---

[7] J.D. Vance, "Opioid of the Masses," *The Atlantic*, July 4, 2016, https://www.theatlantic.com/politics/archive/2016/07/opioid-of-the-masses/489911/.

the real problems of the working-class people. But Vance also worried that Trump was confirming the opinion of these people that the issue is *out there*, that problems were being imposed on them by elites, government, and corrupt institutions rather than by their own bad choices and broken communities. But if the problems are, at their core, coming from the hearts and choices of individuals and from the brokenness of local communities themselves, then Vance worried that Trump was giving false hope that his populist movement could do what it could not: heal these people and their communities of their brokenness.

Vance predicted a possible future where "even with a President Trump, their homes and families are still domestic war zones, their newspapers' obituaries continue to fill with the names of people who died too soon, and their faith in the American Dream continues to falter. But it will come, and when it does, I hope Americans cast their gaze to those with the most power to address so many of these problems: each other." Vance's reflection here was essentially that of a small government Conservative skeptical of federal solutions to local problems. If the major problems of ordinary Americans stem from broken families, bad personal choices, and severed communities, then Trump's rhetoric blaming the carnage on corrupt elites in Washington, DC was inappropriate and would only fuel the tendency of these people to blame others rather than try to fix their own problems. With such a world view, Vance's skepticism of Trump was understandable, if ultimately wrong and a bit naive.

Before discussing the MAGA conversion, it is worth noting that Vance said much more about Trump in his early years than what is expressed in "Opioid of the Masses." In 2016, Vance said "I'm a Never Trump guy.... I never liked him." He referred to

Trump as "an idiot," "noxious," and "reprehensible."[8] Vance was also quoted as saying many other negative things about Trump, including wondering whether Trump was "America's Hitler." But comments that are leaked from private conversations are not really worth addressing, so we will stick with the 2016 material that Vance said or wrote publicly.

There is no use in hiding the obvious truth: Vance said many negative, even vitriolic, things about Trump in 2016. One could excuse these statements as those of a young, inexperienced man new to the political scene. But the issue is worth taking seriously. In 2016, Vance considered himself a "never-Trump" Conservative. A few years later, Vance was a Trump ally and apologist. What happened? The answer is important to understanding why MAGA has taken such a strong hold within the Republican Party and the conservative movement.

What If Trump Is Right?

So in 2016, Vance called Trump an "opioid of the masses" (and much else besides) and explained the basis for his claims. He claimed Trump was a crutch that helped people cope with America's problems but would not solve them. Through many writings and statements made in 2016, Vance seemed convinced that Trump was riding the populist wave with no ability to actually solve the problems of the people he claimed to represent. How did Vance evolve from serious opposition to Trump to being selected as Trump's vice-presidential candidate? As we said earlier, accusations that Vance is simply a political opportunist

---

[8] Allison, Natalie, "'My god what an idiot': J.D. Vance gets whacked for past Trump comments," *Politico*, October 23, 2021, https://www.politico.com/news/2021/10/23/jd-vance-ohio-senate-trump-comments-516865.

fail to take into account that Vance has spoken candidly, and quite convincingly, about why his stance on President Trump changed so dramatically. In 2016, Vance thought that American institutions were in decent shape and that therefore Trump's position and rhetoric were unjustified and unhelpful, even dangerous. So what changed?

Vance gives a very insightful summary of how he came around to President Trump's position within the GOP in a conversation on the New York Times Podcast in October 2024.[9] The NYT interviewer began the conversation by reading some of Vance's past comments critical of President Trump. The interviewer focused particularly on Vance's former view that Trump was dragging down political discourse and "spent way too much time appealing to people's fears." The interviewer asked why Vance is more comfortable with Trump's political approach today; Vance's answer explains his evolution.

When Vance wrote *Hillbilly Elegy* in 2016, he was rather optimistic about the future of America. He thought Trump's focus on the fears of the American people and the negative aspects of American life were excessive, tending to drag people down rather than build them up. But after Trump won the 2016 election, Vance said it was time to reflect on the significance of the American people choosing Trump. As Vance watched the media downplay the legitimate concerns—immigration, trade, and war—that led to the election of Trump, as he watched the media blame Trump's election on racism and Russian interference,

---

[9] "A Conversation with JD Vance," *The Interview | A Podcast from the New York Times,* October 12, 2024, https://www.youtube.com/watch?v=LngsF2T8Ci0.

Vance became more open to the idea that the popular narrative was missing something big.

What Vance slowly learned was that "if you believe the American political culture is fundamentally healthy but may be biased toward the Left, then Donald Trump is not the right solution to that problem." This was Vance's early view: if Trump is stoking unwarranted fears among the American people, he is a danger rather than a solution. If things in America were slanted Left but were fundamentally not so bad, then it is a reasonable conclusion that Donald Trump was a bad figure emerging in American politics.

But as Vance continued to observe political and cultural realities, he "slowly developed a viewpoint that the American political culture was…deeply diseased and the American media conversation had become so deranged that it couldn't even process the frustrations of a large share, maybe even a…majority of the country, then when you say 'well, I don't like Donald Trump's language,' well, Donald Trump's language actually maybe makes a whole lot more sense if you assume that the institutions are much more corrupted than they were before."

There is a lot to reflect on in this exchange. In fact, this short conversation highlights what is probably the biggest divide within the Republican Party today. The disagreements on the Right are perhaps less about the proper role of government or the policy issues to be emphasized and more about the health of America and its institutions. Where are we as a nation? Is the country simply going through a normal cycle, an excessively liberal time that will likely swing back to a saner, more moderate culture in the coming years? Or have most of the nation's institutions—its government agencies, media outlets, universities, and corporations—been captured not merely by Liberals but by radical, un-American Leftists who want to destroy America as we know it? The answer to this drastic question will shape an American Conservative's views on Donald Trump and the direction of the Republican Party.

The divide in the Republican Party may be better explained by one's view of the health of the nation than by "neocon vs. MAGA" policy disagreements. If the former view is correct, if America remains a more or less healthy nation that happens to be guided by more liberal influences at the moment, then the MAGA movement is not the right remedy for what ails us. Why engage in fiery, exaggerated rhetoric, demonize the opposition party, call for the abolition of entire federal agencies, and so on, if all we need is better, more conservative leadership in the next election cycle? One does not need a firehose to put out a candle.

But if the latter view is correct, if we are truly in the grip of advanced cultural decay and even on the brink of national collapse, then Trump and the MAGA shift within the Republican Party are not only understandable but necessary. If partisan operatives run the Department of Justice and the FBI, prosecuting political enemies rather than administering justice, if career bureaucrats are actually impeding the will of the people and their elected leaders, if the media and the universities are trying to manipulate people to hate America and destroy it, if the current leadership and government policies are not only misguided but are intentionally destroying American families and the American economy, then perhaps Republicans in the past several decades have not been the fierce fighters they are called to be in this critical moment in American history.

This distinction explains Vance's shift on Trump. Unlike many politicians who mysteriously changed their priorities and quickly came around to Trump when it became politically expedient to do so, Vance's account of his Trumpian evolution is reasonable. From 2016 to the present, Vance may have grown and become more mature and articulate on certain policies, but he has essentially cared about the same things. He has observed drugs, offshoring of manufacturing jobs, and broken, dysfunctional families destroying American communities and he wants to think seriously about political solutions to these problems. The big change in Vance is that, over the last few years, he has come to believe that American institutions are much more corrupt and dysfunctional than he once thought. This change in Vance's view of America justifies a much more favorable view of Trump's policy priorities, his rhetoric, and his fighting spirit. Trump's policy priorities and take-no-prisoners style is not a crutch for disaffected Americans but actually a needed part of the solution to what ails the nation.

Vance's change in stance toward Donald Trump seems less like political opportunism, or even a change in views on policy, than like a change in Vance's view of the health of America. Vance has been consistently skeptical of Libertarianism, concerned about the plight of the American family, the opioid crisis, and a lack of good, blue-collar manufacturing jobs, both before and after his support of Trump. What *has* changed is that Vance once thought Trump's rhetoric about the state of America was excessively pessimistic and bombastic, but he has now come to believe that American institutions are indeed as bad as Trump and his political allies have been saying for years. Vance's diagnosis of the problems and solutions in American life have not changed much. What has changed drastically is his diagnosis of the institutions that are necessary to effect changes and implement solutions.

So after making these initial general points in the interview, Vance turns to how he personally came around to Trump. Vance realized that Trump's way of speaking—he seems to be constantly attacking opponents—is more productive, perhaps even more necessary, than Vance once thought. By attacking institutions, including members of the political and bureaucratic establishment as well as the media, Trump was able to "illustrate how broken the American political and media culture is right now." If he did not go directly at these institutions, he would not have been able to get anything done because the institutions have such a strong grip on our government and our popular culture. If Trump didn't appear to be waging a rhetorical war, the American people—including Vance—may not have come to realize that such a fight was necessary.

This is the essence of Vance's pro-Trump conversion. "So what I saw in 2016 as a fault of Donald Trump's, by 2018, 2019 I very much saw as an advantage." Vance went from blaming Trump's rhetoric for "driving the divisiveness" in modern political culture to realizing that Trump was "responding to it and giving voice to a group of people who had been completely ignored." This is another key point. What Vance points out here has been a common source of tension and disagreement on the Right in the Trump era. The temptation of many Conservatives is to blame Donald Trump for making the political conversation more crass, for lowering the level of discourse from intelligent political debate to harsh personal statements and made-for-TV sound bites.

But I think people are confusing cause and effect here. Think about the timeline: Twitter came out in 2006 and had 100 million users by 2012. YouTube began in 2005 and by July 2006 had over 100 million views per day. For decades, technology has moved people away from long-form content (books, intellectual debates, and full-length interviews) to shorter and shorter pieces of content (TikTok videos, YouTube shorts, and Twitter/X posts). With the rise of new, short-form content, coupled with algorithms that tend to polarize and give people more and more of what they want, the media landscape has been creating hyper-partisan, caustic political echo chambers for about twenty years now.

The upheaval of American political life was well underway before Trump stepped off the escalator in 2015. Whatever one thinks of Trump, the man has amazing media instincts. He saw the issues that were plaguing ordinary, working-class Americans and understood better than anyone else in the political scene what it would take to capture the minds and hearts of the millions of Americans who felt forgotten and left behind by the political elites. It is more accurate to say that Trump understood and took advantage of the state of modern political discourse than to say that he caused it.

There are two important takeaways from Vance's comments on Trump. First, Vance should be admired for his humility. Many politicians have flipped from anti-Trump to MAGA for political expediency, leaving old views and political positions behind as if they were never held. Vance's move toward Trump does not involve the hypocrisy of pretending that he was never really anti-Trump, nor does it involve a flip-flop on core principles. Vance cared about the same problems in America in 2016, 2020, and 2024. And he admits that he changed. But as his view of the health of America shifted, so too did his view of what it would take to fix things.

Second, Vance acknowledges that while Trump's style was a necessary and effective reaction to the state of American institutions, he does not need to mimic that style.

> President Trump's approach is President Trump's approach. His style is his style. Do I think that his style and his approach is a necessary corrective to what's broken about American society? Yes, I do. That doesn't mean I'm going to be Donald Trump because…nobody can be Donald Trump. I think he is a uniquely interesting, charismatic figure but it's just not who I am. Fundamentally he and I are going to have different styles.

Vance is open about the fact that he is not Donald Trump. He does not have the same charisma nor the same style. That admission reveals a strength of JD Vance: he is not primarily a charismatic TV personality. He is a public intellectual, which is clear from his writings, his media appearances, and the way he gives campaign speeches and presents his policy ideas. This is important and encouraging for the future of the Republican Party post-Trump. As Vance explained in his speech at *The American Conservative* in 2019, Trump's excellent political instincts started a massive change within the party and the country, but those instincts alone are "not enough to build a political movement around."[10] Vance has spent years now as a political thinker, a reader of political philosophy, and a public writer. He may be less charismatic and more "nerdy" than Trump, but he has the right instincts and depth of thought about policy to be the leader that helps the new Republican Party navigate the post-Trump years.

---

[10] Sen. J.D. Vance, "Towards a Pro-Worker, Pro-Family Conservatism," *The American Conservative*, May 29, 2019, https://www.theamericanconservative.com/towards-a-pro-worker-pro-family-conservatism/.

So what is the takeaway from Vance's change in stance toward Donald Trump over the years? Vance is clear and humble about the shift. Vance's views on American society have changed. Trump was right and, in a way, Vance was wrong (or at least a bit naive) in 2016. Vance is consistent in his views about the problems that any serious conservative politics needs to address, but he has evolved to realize that the problems are much more deeply embedded in American institutions than he thought in 2016.

As a result, Vance has come to believe that Trump's rhetoric, his rather intense manner of calling out and attacking those who oppose him, are not a dangerous liability or weakness. In fact, Trump's attitude may be the best way to draw attention to the depth of the problems and to get people to understand the serious work it will take to fix those problems.

That being said, Vance is not Trump—nobody is Trump. Vance may now share Trump's views of the dark state of affairs in American institutions, but Vance is no shoot-from-the-hip TV personality. Vance possesses a brilliant mind, a deep grasp of political philosophy and policy, and the political skills necessary to handle the greatest problems of American life. This, coupled with his position as Trump's vice president and heir apparent, positions Vance to be the leader of the post-Trump Republican Party.

VII

Beyond Libertarianism

The previous chapters have laid the foundation of who JD Vance is: a brilliant but ultimately normal American guy; the model of the American dream; a political intellectual; a Conservative who has only in recent years realized the depths of the problems that plague America. Now it is time to turn to what Vance thinks about politics.

Vance has frequently called for a more robust conservatism that is not shy about using government power for the common good. This call is based largely on his view of the state of American culture and institutions. In a healthy society, a small, restrained, hands-off government may be all that is necessary for the nation to thrive. But times are bad, the nation's institutions are poisoned, and so the Right is justified in this unique time to use government action to achieve goods that would be reserved to private institutions in saner times.

While that is true and is clearly a key part of Vance's thinking about American politics today, it does not tell the whole story of Vance and the new forms of conservatism gaining momentum within the modern Republican Party. Yes, some of these changes are coming from a "desperate times" rationale. But not all of them. In fact, there is a philosophical break from Libertarianism taking place within the modern Right. There are many Conservatives, and Vance is certainly one of them, who think that Libertarianism is not only inadequate for our times, but is objectively an inadequate political philosophy that should not govern the thinking of the Republican Party.

What Is Libertarianism and Why Does It Matter?

Before diving into Vance's criticisms of Libertarianism and its effects on the Republican Party, it is worth a quick sketch of what Libertarianism is and the role it has played in the Republican Party over the last several decades.

Libertarianism has many definitions; the philosophical roots and various branches of Libertarianism go far beyond the scope of this book. But a simple summary is that it is a political philosophy that emphasizes individual rights, individual freedom of choice, and minimal government control over individuals, the free market, and life in general. Libertarians, for both philosophical and practical reasons, generally believe that government planning and government intervention almost always produce a worse outcome than if the private choices of individuals were left unrestrained in a free market.

It should be noted that Libertarians are not anarchists, so most Libertarians accept that at least some government is necessary to prevent chaos. This makes it a bit difficult to draw the line between what is legitimate government action and what is unacceptable overreach that would best be left in the hands of private individuals and institutions. But for present purposes, it should suffice to say that Libertarianism is a political philosophy that has a default preference for individual liberty and autonomy and a suspicion of government solutions to most societal problems.

Why does Libertarianism matter? Isn't this just a philosophical quibble for right-wing intellectuals to debate about? The question is relevant for practical politics because the tension between Libertarianism and Conservatism within the Republican Party has seriously affected how the party has campaigned and governed for decades. According to Vance and many within the modern American conservative movement, an excessive deference to Libertarianism in the modern Republican Party has created great problems. A libertarian philosophy of politics and government has led to a conservative movement that has often failed to use government power to address serious problems. Critics of Libertarianism in the modern Republican Party, including Vance, fear that Libertarianism is not up to the task of tackling the serious political and social problems that threaten our nation.

JD Vance: Beyond Libertarianism

In 2019, Vance spoke to the National Conservatism conference on the limits of (and his disagreements with) Libertarianism.[11] Vance began by recounting his vision of the American dream before discussing how Libertarianism fails to address the root

---

[11] "J. D. Vance: Beyond Libertarianism - National Conservatism Conference," Speech by JD Vance, July 16, 2021, posted July 19, 2021, by National Conservatism. YouTube. https://www.youtube.com/watch?v=dmVjKIEC8rw.

problems of America because it fails to address the true and proper measures of success.

Hillbilly Elegy, and modern politics in general, is about the decline of the American dream. That decline is not a decline of material wealth and consumption. It is a decline of the family caused by abusive homes, drugs, the decay of communities, the collapse of American manufacturing, and "the loss of dignity and purpose and meaning that come along with" the crumbling of families and communities. Vance's American dream is simply to have a meaningful job to support a family and to be a good husband and father. This is quite different from what is often characterized as the American dream: to be more materially successful than one's parents (better schools, more prestigious jobs and awards, and more money) and for one's children to do the same. Both versions of the dream share a hope that each generation can be more successful than the one before it, but the criteria for success are quite different.

Vance links this difference in visions of the American dream to a distinction between libertarian politics and conservative politics. Vance defines Libertarianism as the view that "so long as public outcomes and social goods are produced by free individual choices, we shouldn't be too concerned about what those goods ultimately produce." What is the problem with letting people choose whatever they want to choose? Vance gives the example of neuroscientists, who will make much more money working for tech companies and developing ways to addict children to smart phones and apps than if they work to cure Alzheimer's. Is that a free choice and a consequence of labor being sold based on its market value? Yes. *But is it good?* Vance argues that we should not submit our economic and social policy thinking to such a system of thought, one that prefers freedom in the market to *what is good*. "We should be concerned that our economy is geared more toward developing applications than curing terrible diseases. We should care about a whole host of public goods, and should actually be willing to use politics and political power to accomplish some of those public goods."

Vance is right to challenge this mantra of freedom and choice. Decades of libertarian dominance on the Right have led to a confusion between means and ends. Freedom and individual choice are *means*. Powerful means, yes. For people to make good and meaningful choices, they generally need to be free from coercion. But the freedom to choose is not itself the good that society exists to foster. It should be fairly obvious that not all free choices are good choices. Why are we free to own guns? Not because freedom to own guns is good, but because it is good to fulfill one's duty to defend one's family and one's neighbors from evil. We value free speech in order that truth might be spoken. We value religious freedom so that people might worship God in spirit and in truth. Freedom is so important because of the good things it allows us to choose, not because it is a good in itself.

For Vance, this is not a merely theoretical problem. He grew up in a community devastated by opioids. When parents are addicts and create an environment where their kids are likely to follow suit and become addicts as well, is that simply an area of life beyond government control? Is the freedom to choose drug use a good thing? Or does the government have a role here to promote the common good? When the government sits back, allows opioid drugs to be commercialized, under regulated, and prescribed and sold too freely, isn't that a political problem, not merely a case where individuals need to make better choices?

Another common clash between conservatism and Libertarianism is the off-shoring of manufacturing jobs. From a libertarian economic perspective, off-shoring makes sense. If businesses are free to choose to manufacture goods in places where labor is cheapest, then things are produced as efficiently as possible and Americans get things at the cheapest prices possible. Yes, this is technically the result of free markets and free choices. But what about the American communities that have lost their biggest employers and now suffer from a lack of good manufacturing jobs? What about the slave-like labor conditions in third-world countries that have replaced American manufacturing? Is the choice to trade these jobs away into the global economy for the sake of freedom and economic efficiency worth the devastation it has caused?

Loose opioid regulation and globalization of the economy were political choices. Are they good simply because they allow private choices to be made free from government interference?

Yes, freedom and individual choice are important. But if freedom is put on a pedestal as a good in itself, we are often choosing to leave people in communities lacking good jobs, ravaged by drugs, and torn apart by these political decisions for so-called freedom. These are political decisions, not requirements of freedom. Leaving individuals and communities subject to the choices of drug companies and transnational corporations is a political *choice*. Allowing private actors to make decisions that are bad for many people in the name of "freedom" does not leave Americans with very good options from which to freely choose.

Another important example Vance points out is the libertarian choice to allow free access to pornography on the internet. As the studies come out showing how pornography warps young minds, we see some disturbing correlations: fewer marriages, fewer children, fewer healthy relationships, and a rise in actual pornography addiction and the resulting sexual dysfunction.

Vance highlights that this too is a political choice: the choice to value freedom—the freedom to access pornography—over promoting "public good like marriage and family and happiness." These are not inevitabilities in a free country; these are *choices*. This is particularly clear in the case of pornography. Obscenity has historically been an exception to the right to free speech and has been banned and punishable by law for most of American history. Our free American society was not founded on a belief that freedom is unlimited; freedom is not meant to be an opportunity to pursue vice. A conception of freedom as license to indulge vices like pornography is a modern novelty. Such a false understanding of freedom is foreign and unacceptable to American conservatism. Conservatives should realize that they can make different political choices moving forward. Freedom for its own sake is not conservative. It is not necessary or inevitable for Conservatives to always choose freedom over government action.

What are modern Americans choosing with all their freedom? People are using their freedom to choose not to have children; America does not have enough babies each year to replace its own population. That may be a free choice, but it is a choice that does not produce a healthy society. Vance points out that the libertarian response seems to be acceptance of the personal choice. We must respect the free choice of modern Americans, who prefer using their time and money taking vacations and acquiring stuff rather than raising children. Vance does address the plummeting fertility rate on libertarian terms: a thriving free economy relies on at least replacement-level reproduction to continue to thrive. Without enough babies, there will not be enough workers and entrepreneurs, and the libertarian utopia will be impossible. But Vance is also clear that we must go beyond economic arguments that would satisfy Libertarians. Society should not promote family formation and children merely due to the economic benefits. The choice to have children creates extended families, community connections, and religious faith. Children are not only useful and necessary cogs in the economic machine. *They are good.*

We must confront the fact that our current circumstances—from falling birth rates to offshoring American manufacturing—are the result of choices. And the choice not to use political power to achieve goods such as healthy family formation is in fact a political choice. These choices are creating a social crisis. If people are addicted to technology, not forming families, and more depressed, anxious, and suicidal than we have seen in any other period in American history, we need to consider the legal and political choices that may be available to address and reverse these devastating trends.

The ultimate question we face is: what end does politics serve? Is the goal to create a free market, to provide as many free choices for individuals as possible? Or does government exercise power to achieve goods deeper than freedom and commerce? We need to choose what goods we serve and what goods we want our government to serve.

As the conservative movement in America begins to question its libertarian orthodoxies—which it has been doing, especially in the last decade—it needs intelligent and prudent leaders. There is a danger of swinging in the opposite direction and attempting to hyperregulate the economy and society in an effort to promote right-wing goals. Government intervention, however well-intentioned toward the common good, can indeed fail to produce its intended effect, and have unintended effects. JD Vance serves as a hopeful figure in the movement to formulate and implement a new conservatism in America. He is deeply skeptical of big government and so he is unlikely to embrace a right-wing version of big government statism. But he also recognizes that twenty-first century America has problems that a hands-off libertarian Republican Party is unequipped to address. So having a figure like Vance willing to entertain creative policy ideas to encourage family formation, the return of American manufacturing, and other solutions to major problems is a sign of hope for the future of the Republican Party.

The Health of America

In *Beyond Libertarianism,* Vance began to develop one of his most important and consistent themes: globalist economics may have lifted many out of poverty and provided more material wealth and comfort for many, but it is not an unqualified success. Conservatives need to face the realities and the problems caused by worship of the free market. Vance elaborated on this theme in his 2019 essay *The Health of Nations,* published at the National Review.[12]

Vance notes that we must acknowledge "the tensions between our pro-market principles and everything else." When pro-market apologists talk about free-market economics producing longer lives, more comfort, fewer dead children, and more living parents, Vance points out a problem: this isn't true. "Our economy has not produced fewer dead children and more living parents in America, at least not in the section of the country where I live. The opioid epidemic, in particular, has ravaged whole communities...." Goods in the stores may be cheaper and the GDP higher

---

[12] JD Vance, "The Health of Nations," *National Review,* January 7, 2019, https://www.nationalreview.com/2019/01/tucker-carlson-health-of-nations-markets/.

in modern America. Fewer people may live in abject material poverty. But this is not the whole story about the state of the American economy. People are dying deaths of despair, addicted and overdosing, in staggering numbers. Perhaps there are metrics other than the freedom of the market, the price of goods, and the gross domestic product that American Conservatives should be concerned with.

Vance uses the opioid epidemic to raise two interesting and important questions. First, he notes that free-market champions, quick to point out that "government intervention" is a bad solution to private sector problems like the opioid epidemic, must confront the fact that bad regulation and patent policy led to the pharmaceutical companies' ability to sell opioids to the masses in the first place. Sometimes the dreaded "government intervention" is actually not an unreasonable imposition on individual liberty, but an opportunity to remedy a problem actually caused by laissez-faire policies and to promote the common good. The free market alone did not lead to the widespread sale and abuse of opioids; there were government choices involved. There always are.

Second, Vance identifies a key problem for modern libertarian-leaning thinkers: "what happens when the companies that drive the market economy—and all of its benefits—don't care about the American nation's social fabric? What happens when, as in the case of a few massive narcotics sellers, they profit by destroying that fabric? Surely our response can't be: 'Well, the market will take care of it.' The market is not a Platonic deity...." The market is not a rational actor; it cannot solve all human problems. Further, when keeping the market free from government interference is the only goal, there is a real danger of overlooking how big, powerful, and dangerous private corporations have become. As Sohrab Ahmari points out in *Tyranny, Inc.*[13], it is a dangerous belief that the only entity capable of tyranny is the government. Major corporations are quite capable of self-serving tyrannical actions that inhibit individual liberty.

In the name of a free market, America has allowed companies to distribute pornography to our children, "gene-edit" human babies to cooperate with the Chinese surveillance state, and legalize and sell recreational marijuana and other drugs. These destructive realities are all justified by adherence to the goal of maintaining the free market because each of these things is caused by private entities seeking profits uninhibited by government interference. But Vance asks whether it is not the role of our laws and our government to prevent such harmful decisions by private actors. These things—pornography, drugs, and so on—are *not good*. A cry of "small government!" every time someone proposes a conservative government intervention is an inadequate response to the serious issues that plague our nation.

The free market is not bad. But it is a tool, not a god. The free market is inadequate if we make it our primary political concern or value. If "we care about the flourishing of our society, and if we value ends besides a larger GDP, then we have to do the difficult work of balancing the competing demands of our values." GDP growth and cheaper goods are one consideration, but not the only one. Healthy families, unaddicted children, and jobs with good wages deserve a voice at the policy table as well. Vance and the future GOP will not obsessively defend "the market" above the rights of healthy citizens, children, families, and communities. Nor should they. The idea that free markets will

---

[13] Sohrab Ahmari, *Tyranny, Inc.: How Private Power Crushed American Liberty—and What to Do About It* (Penguin Random House, 2023).

solve the problem of what is best for the nation "is a recipe for boring thinking and bad policy."

Vance intimately understands the various entrenched camps on economic issues on the Right—the committed classical Liberals/Libertarians who lean toward Ayn Rand anarcho-capitalism, as well as the post-Liberals who don't care much for defending the free market at all. But Vance does not seem to be a theoretical adherent to either camp. He clearly thinks that free markets with open and fair competition between all comers, unburdened by unnecessary government regulation and oversight, are generally a good thing. Government manipulation of markets often leads to cronyism, monopolies, or things being made and sold less efficiently. But Vance and the modern Right have grown rightfully skeptical of elevating noninterference in the market from a generally good idea to a dogma.

Yes, usually unregulated competition on the free market is a good thing for America. But not always and not in all situations. There are times when matters of national security, concern for the American workers' wages, the health of citizens, or a number of other concerns require fealty to the free market to take a back seat to other concerns. It is important to watch that government economic regulation does not cause more problems than it solves. But skepticism of government action should not lead to the erroneous idea that government action is always bad or improper for a Conservative to support. Vance is a model of this "free markets are good, but not the highest good" philosophy that is so important to ensuring that twenty-first century American conservatism balances the tensions between political theories and real issues.

Vance ends *The Health of America* with an insight that runs consistently through his writing over the years, goes beyond political philosophy, and touches the heart of a tension, almost a paradox. There is "a tension between acknowledging adversity and fighting to overcome it." In *Hillbilly Elegy*, Vance recounts the way his Mamaw acknowledged that the world was not fair. At the same time, she warned JD that he could *never* become the kind of person who gave up and didn't work hard because the world was not fair. Yes, there is adversity that comes from forces beyond an individual's control; individual choices and hard work can overcome many of these adverse conditions. Policy may be able to help address these issues as well as individual choice. Both these things are true, so both personal excellence and policy intervention are appropriate to create a better nation and promote the common good.

Therefore, the encouragement of good individual choices in a free market is essential to a healthy society—the Libertarians are onto something. But there are some circumstances where government policy has a key role in helping make better options available for individuals to choose. Here Vance breaks from hard Libertarianism. Freedom is important, but people should not be free from government interference in order to make whatever decisions they please. This supposed freedom leaves many destructive options on the table, options that government has a legitimate interest in preventing—addiction to dangerous drugs or the shipping of good American blue-collar jobs overseas. Here, Conservatives need to offer something more than freedom from government intervention. Conservatives need to propose positive solutions for the common good, even if they restrict certain freedoms, so that people have better choices to make.

The philosophical tension within the modern Right between Conservatives and staunch Libertarians has real effects on the way the Republican Party is able to campaign, craft its message, and govern. Having someone like Vance at the helm, who has thoughtful disagreements with Libertarianism while still maintaining a healthy skepticism of big government and a love for liberty, is important as the party reorients itself around families and workers while still including Libertarians within its coalition.

VIII

A New Conservatism: Workers and Families

The Republican Party of previous decades was often labeled the party of the billionaire, the party of the wealthy, and the party of big corporations. While that claim was often exaggerated or misused for rhetorical purposes, it probably had some merit. But the claim has become increasingly outdated. The Republican Party has moved away from being the party of the wealthy corporate class. As corporations and wealthy, college educated Americans broke to the Left in the Trump era, the Republican Party has realigned dramatically. While this realignment is still ongoing and the effect will not be fully comprehended for years to come, it is becoming clear that the target demographic of the new Republican Party is the working class and the family.

In 2019, Vance published *Towards a Pro-Worker, Pro-Family Conservatism*[14] at *The American Conservative*. The essay, adapted from a speech, feels pivotal, as if Vance is just beginning to move from a public writer/commentator to a man of influence in politics and the conservative movement. Vance begins by explaining the reason he wrote *Hillbilly Elegy* in the first place. The purpose was to explore why so many people from his family and his community (including himself) "had lost faith in what we call the American dream." This topic is one of Vance's core themes; the loss of the American dream is the very idea that led him into public life, into politics, and now into the vice presidency.

The American dream meant generations of Americans striving for a good, successful, and glorious life; now that dream seems to be fading. Why? For most of American history, each generation has been extremely optimistic about America's future and the future of the next generation. It seems this negative generational change is widespread and is not limited to Vance's family or community. A 2023 Pew Research poll shows that "Americans are more pessimistic than optimistic about many aspects of the country's future."[15] What happened to depress the American dream? Vance reflects on disadvantage—on growing up around so much poverty, addiction, abuse, violence, and general disorder—and wonders what happened to the American optimism that always thought the next generation would have

---

[14] Sen. J.D. Vance, "Towards a Pro-Worker, Pro-Family Conservatism," *The American Conservative*, May 29, 2019, https://www.theamericanconservative.com/towards-a-pro-worker-pro-family-conservatism/.

[15] Alexandra Cahn and Kiley Hurst, "Americans Are More Pessimistic than Optimistic About Many Aspects of the Country's Future," *Pew Research*, September 18, 2023, https://www.pewresearch.org/short-reads/2023/09/18/americans-are-more-pessimistic-than-optimistic-about-many-aspects-of-the-countrys-future/.

it better than the last. But social mobility has stagnated, fewer people are doing better than their parents, and there is less hope in the air. This general malaise is what motivated Vance to move into politics and seek solutions.

Vance moves from one of his key themes (the difficulty of social mobility) to another related one: the tension between personal and social responsibility for the nation's ills. Where "does personal responsibility begin and where does responsibility of the broader community end?" Vance recognizes that this tension does not fit neatly into the framework of either the modern Right or the modern Left, but that solving it is key to saving the American dream. The Right is skeptical of government programs meant to remedy social problems, while the Left tends to dislike libertarian-sounding arguments that blame societal problems on individual choices and lack of personal responsibility. Working out this tension rather than playing to either extreme is a necessary task for the modern Republican Party. Creatively responding to the tension between individualism and the role of government in achieving the common good is something that Vance has been quite willing to engage with, even at the cost of breaking with some Republican orthodoxies.

While there are many examples of the societal dysfunctions that hinder the American dream—dysfunctions that Vance posits may be bigger than individual choices can fix—he uses one particular anecdote several times in his writings. He once spoke to a youth counselor from his region in Ohio who worked with an eight-year-old boy with an opioid addiction. Yes, a drug-addicted eight-year-old child. This child had drug-addict parents, of course, who fed their own addictions by dealing drugs. The parents would have the child deliver drugs for them and he would sometimes be "rewarded" with a Vicodin pill. This is a horrifying problem, a tragedy indicative of a society that is deeply sick. But what is the answer?

Vance talks first about the Left and its suggestions that better job opportunities and better educational opportunities would solve these societal problems. If that child's parents were better educated and could find other work, they wouldn't have to resort to dealing drugs. The Right talks about personal responsibility and smarter choices as the remedy. The parents are free people with agency. They chose drugs; they can also make the hard choice to stop and create a better life for themselves and their son. Both responses to the situation are deficient. A society in which parents are hooked on drugs, are using their child to help sell drugs to fund their addiction, and who give that small child drugs as a "reward," has bigger problems than jobs, schools, and personal virtue. Federal and state programs have dumped money into these broken school districts. There have been periods—especially in the post-COVID economy—where wages rose and jobs became readily available in these communities. There have been campaigns and programs for decades encouraging people to rise above drug abuse and make better choices. These are all good things, but they do not address the heart of the matter.

Where is the healthy family and strong community that is necessary to prevent such a terrible personal and familial breakdown? The institutions and communities we live in do more than influence us: in a real way, they shape our view of "what's possible to us." Yes, we need to exercise personal responsibility. But growing up with drug-addicted parents, abusive relationships, and neighborhoods where everyone is living more or less the same way does not form kids who even know *what personal responsibility is*, let alone kids who have the capacity to make good choices. Children in such environments have none of the tools, habits, or examples that make good choices likely.

Vance criticizes the Left for talking as if disadvantaged people have no control and no agency over their life and their future choices. He talks about the importance of creating a culture of hope within the conservative conversation that encourages even the very disadvantaged to see themselves as having hope, optimism, and control over their decisions for the future. Bleeding-heart Liberals tend to blame the system while excusing the problematic individual as a victim. This doesn't help. If those in the depths of poverty, addiction, relationship instability, or violence are continually treated as if they have a terminal illness causing their problems, they start to believe it. These ills are inflicted on them from without; how could they possibly live any differently? When you keep telling people they are helpless and cannot improve their situation, they start to believe it and will never work to improve their situation.

But Vance also rightly criticizes many Conservatives for "ignoring the role that politics must play in giving that kid a better shot and a better chance at his dreams." For most Americans, those dreams are not (or should not be) wealth or fame, but rather the opportunity to be a good spouse and a good parent with a good, meaningful job to provide for a family. This reframing of the American dream is an important contribution to modern conservative discourse: Vance is speaking not of "the American dream of the strivers" but "the American dream of a fulfilled and happy and simple, but I think a very pure and very decent life." Conservatives need to understand politics and government as a tool to promote that good, pure, decent life for as many of its people as possible. When the poor and disadvantaged dream of climbing out of their difficult circumstances, we should encourage that possibility and long for it. But we should remind folks that the better circumstances they seek should be better, happier homes with a loving spouse, children, and decent work, not luxury cars, flashy clothes, and the enviable life of the Instagram influencer. We need a politics that helps lift people up to the American dream, but it needs to be the right dream.

Viewed from that corrected angle, the American crisis is not simply about jobs and wages, but about an epidemic of drugs, domestic violence and trauma, and the absence of stable marriages and families. Yes, Vance experienced these things in an intense way, but sadly he is not much of an outlier. Marriage rates are down, single-parent families are increasingly the norm, and drugs and domestic abuse are not a rare exception in American households today. These trends have increased in recent decades, even when the economy is good.

Vance asks the simple, obvious question that all who care about politics and the common good need to ask: "What do we do about that?" Tax cuts, corporate deregulation, and admonishment to "make better choices" are not sufficient. Libertarianism is not a conservative politics that rises to the challenges and realities of the day. Frequent divorce and the scourge of parents not sufficiently involved in the lives of their children will not be solved by higher wages alone. There is a fertility crisis that is now becoming an issue as American birth rates have plummeted below replacement levels. Societies with fewer children, and particularly fewer children growing up in attentive, loving homes, have "less innovation, less dynamism, they're less stable societies." As we have more retirement-aged people and fewer children, we no longer have a functional social safety net nor a sufficient number of future citizens to make this nation work.

Even Libertarians need to care deeply about the family crisis, because the economic impacts will be severe.

But the social result is more important than the economic impact. Men who do not grow into fathers are more likely to be restless, aimless, and lost. People without children have a harder time being involved, productive members of their communities because they are not raising the next generation for whom they want to ensure the community thrives. Adult human beings long to be a parent, both biologically and spiritually. It is good to have children, then grandchildren, so that society grows, ages, and continues on in the healthy, natural progression of generations. We should care about the decline of fertility rates and stable families not only because we need a population to have a society, but because, on a fundamental level, Conservatives "think babies are good, and we think babies are good because we're not sociopaths."

In 2019, Vance already had his finger on the problem facing the Republican Party in the years to come. At the time of this speech, he hesitated to lay out the entire conservative platform for the coming years for a reason. The realignment around families and workers was new and the details still needed to be worked out. That is still true today. Republicans "still need to figure out a lot of the details for how this vision of conservative politics, a pro-family, pro-worker, pro-American nation, conservatism actually looks in practice." This is a humble admission and an important insight. It is extremely difficult to figure out how to translate these priorities (supporting families, workers, and the interests of America over the rest of the world) into particular policy solutions. But these are the guiding principles that Conservatives need to focus on. How do we craft *every* policy proposal in *every* area of politics and government to promote strong, stable families, good jobs for ordinary Americans, and a nation loved by its citizens? It is a hard question that libertarian-minded Conservatives have been a bit allergic to for decades. But it is the question Republicans need to ask for the future of the party and the good of the country. If there are problems that Republican policy has not adequately addressed but that we realize now need addressing, it is time to talk. It may even be time to experiment. Policies should be debated and tried to make the lives of workers and families better. The platform will be fleshed out as the party embraces the reality of its new base and the problems of the day.

Vance is admittedly painting with a broad brush here. In 2019, he was just starting the work of outlining how these pro-family, pro-worker principles should become policy proposals. But Vance did touch on some key themes in this piece, themes that the party has been working to develop over the past few years to realign as the party of the worker and the family.

First, economic Libertarianism can be problematic to the national interest, because large corporations are now multinational or global. The leadership and shareholders have no incentive to look out for the interests of American workers or citizens. Worrying about government tyranny while allowing international corporations, completely unchecked by regulation, to grow to the size and strength of nations is a problem. As we have seen tech companies silence political stories and deplatform major public figures, it is clear that Libertarianism does not have an adequate answer to the problem of the tyranny of large private corporations.

Second, immigration policy in America can be generous and acknowledge the benefits of immigrants to society, but the policies must be in the interests of (not to the detriment of) current American workers. An immigration system that hurts the citizens and the workers already here in America, either by allowing in too much economic competition or simply by ceasing to function at all, is broken. As Vance said on *Face the Nation* in January 2025, we need to make sure that we don't let American myths and stories about being a nation of immigrants prevent us from making common sense policy decisions about immigration: "This is a very unique country, and it was founded by some immigrants and some settlers. But just because we were founded by immigrants, doesn't mean that 240 years later we have to have the dumbest immigration policy in the world."[16]

Third, foreign policy needs to focus on a strong America that keeps the nation safe and secure, but does not use the lives of American military members to serve "imperial hubris." The interest of America is in defending and securing America. Nothing more, nothing less.

Finally, while "family policy" is a broad and sometimes vague term, a coherent conservative politics needs to work to ensure that we will continue to have an America where future generations will have hope in the American dream, a reasonable hope for a decent job, a happy family, and a safe, vibrant community.

Vance was quite right that, as the Republican Party develops its platform for the years and decades to come, it should focus on the American family and the American worker. He posits a question that Conservatives should ask as they reevaluate what a pro-worker, pro-family Conservative movement will actually

---

[16] Tim Hains, "VP VANCE: Just Because We Were Founded by Immigrants, Doesn't Mean 240 Years Later We Need the Dumbest Immigration Policy," *Face the Nation*, January 26, 2025, https://www.realclearpolitics.com/video/2025/01/26/vp_vance_just_because_we_were_founded_by_immigrants_doesnt_mean_240_years_later_we_need_the_dumbest_immigration_policy.html.

look like. We need to "focus our minds and our efforts on who we're for. Who are we for as Conservatives? It's not just commercial interests." Conservatives are for a lot of people. We are for the heroic citizens who step up, help their families (like Vance's Mamaw), and change the lives of those who might otherwise be lost and without assistance. We are for families who are struggling to raise children in a world where children are seen more and more as an inconvenient, optional choice. This includes large families; it includes single mothers who chose life and are struggling against incredible odds to raise their children. We need to be "for good mothers and the dreams of their children."

Vance rightly credits President Trump for opening up new ways of re-thinking everything from foreign policy to immigration to trade. But he also makes a key insight, one that motivated the writing of this book and that explains why Vance stands as such an important figure in a critical time: "one of the lessons of the Trump presidency…is that a politician with good instincts on issues like trade is not enough to build a political movement around." Trump is the beginning of something big; he is not the end of it. We need people who will take the realignment that Trump has started, a rethinking of the political coalitions and policy issues that form the Republican Party, and move it forward. We need a conservatism that can develop what Trump started into a comprehensive, coherent, intellectual way of thinking about politics based on supporting American families and American workers. That work has begun through the efforts of some excellent think tanks, publications, and political figures in recent years who were willing to acknowledge that a new era is dawning in America and in Republic party politics. JD Vance is at the very center of it. The way in which Vance, Trump's chosen successor to lead the party and the MAGA movement, has developed his thinking on politics, government, and policy centered on the American worker. The American family will be central to the direction that the Republican Party takes in the years to come.

Vance the Senate Candidate: New Role, Same Priorities

Two years after the speech for The American Conservative, Vance gave another important political speech—this one to the Intercollegiate Studies Institute. The speech was published as an essay at *The American Conservative* as "A Civilizational Crisis"[17] in July 2021. This is a foundational essay in Vance's political life, because of both the topic and the timing. Vance officially announced his campaign for the US Senate on July 1, 2021. He gave this speech three weeks later, focusing on important issues of politics and family policy. At the time of the previous speech, Vance had not been a politician, but had laid out the need for the Republican Party to start fleshing out the details of what a pro-worker, pro-family, and America First party platform would look like. In this speech, one of Vance's first as a political candidate, he takes the issue up again.

Vance begins his remarks by calling for courage, particularly within the conservative movement. This call to courage, which can mean several things, is a needed reminder for those who delve into politics. Courage can mean standing up against the errors of the Left and publicly proclaiming conservative principles that may be unpopular. But it can also mean the courage to

---

[17] Sen. J.D. Vance, "A Civilizational Crisis," *The American Conservative*, July 27, 2021, https://www.theamericanconservative.com/a-civilizational-crisis/.

introduce new, creative ways of thinking that are not popular or acceptable within conservative circles. Both standing up to the Left and standing up to the Right can be needed instances of political courage; both are habits found in JD Vance.

From the moment Vance was declared Trump's running mate, he was labeled everything from "too extreme" to "weird." He boldly went on every hostile morning show he could and tirelessly interviewed on subjects from abortion to immigration. He showed great courage in standing up to the Left. But at the same time, Vance has been a bold voice unafraid to challenge Republican orthodoxies. He has pushed back against the free-market orthodoxies that refuse to use government power to curb excesses or problems that come from unstrained private economic actors. He was one of the first vocal skeptics of funding Ukraine in its war effort against Russia, despite the initial pro-Ukraine hawkishness of most Republicans in Congress. Vance has demonstrated that the courage he called for when he first began his run for public office was not an empty word but a virtue that he himself takes seriously in his political life.

Vance tells the story of the first time he began to understand the courage that would be demanded of a conservative public figure. He made public comments about the demographic crisis and the need for more babies. That statement was picked up by the *Washington Post* and misconstrued to mean the nation needs more *white* babies. Vance did not say that, of course. But nevertheless, the headline spread and Vance lost business. He lost professional contacts. His livelihood was threatened as a result of this media attack. He realized then that courage is necessary in this civilizational fight—one cannot speak and act on these important and often controversial issues in the public square and expect to take no hits in the process. He also realized the importance of friendship to foster courage. We cannot take these bold stands alone. The conservative movement ought not to be merely a coalition of thinkers or political actors, but a group of friends ready and willing to support one another in what can sometimes become a tough and nasty fight. Yes, we need a network so we can find work and professional support in the event that one of our own is "canceled." But more important, we need friends fighting the fight with us so that we remember we are not alone. It is easy to become discouraged in a battle if one thinks one is fighting it alone.

In this speech, Vance returns to his theme of the American dream and gives perhaps his most simple and concise definition of the term: the American dream is "about a good life in your own country." And again, this good life is not about lots of money and consuming lots of material goods. The good life is as simple as the ability to be a good spouse and a good parent, and to have meaningful work to provide for a family. Vance's emphasis on this point is worth repeating consistently, because it animates the way he thinks about all political issues. Politics and government should be about nothing more than fostering a good society where people can have good family lives, good jobs, and a simple, happy life. Everything from foreign policy to tax policy should be centered around this basic goal of making stable, happy lives for as many American families as possible.

What does this "good spouse, good parent, meaningful work" ideal look like in practice? Vance offers two components. The first component is economic. In a healthy nation, people who work hard and do what they are supposed to do should be able to "support a middle-class family on a single wage." Policies on immigration, trade, and manufacturing should not focus primarily on cheap goods but on ensuring more of the American middle class can achieve this standard of living.

The second component is cultural: "to live a good life in your own country, you have to actually feel respected. And you have to be able to teach your children to honor and love the things that you were taught to honor and love." The country needs to be fundamentally patriotic. This is not about patriotic trappings, "flag waving and Fourth of July parades," but something much deeper. It means that the people love and appreciate the accomplishments and the greatness of their homeland.

Vance frames this deep need for patriotism as a political problem because of the serious ways in which the modern left has undermined citizens' healthy love and appreciation of America. This attack has come fundamentally as an assault on history. The way many American schools teach children and many mainstream media outlets speak about history has shifted radically in recent decades. The American founding is not taught as one of the greatest political accomplishments in history, but rather as a history of white men founding a country on slavery and genocide. The Pilgrims' amazing arrival in Massachusetts, their survival of brutal winters and harsh conditions to begin the founding of America has been replaced by stories of the mistreatment and displacement of Native Americans. These choices are not mere differences in emphasis. When people are taught (from kindergarten through adulthood) that America's origins are evil and our history is nothing but enslavement, racism, and genocide, they are not merely hearing one side of the story. This is propaganda that makes it nearly impossible for citizens to love America. A patriotic civics education does not need to ignore the dark realities of history; but it certainly should not pretend that America is *nothing but* these dark realities.

Vance makes clear that how we understand the past shapes the future. This re-education program implemented by the Left is "not about correcting systemic racism or systemic wrong. It's about making us easier to control." This is a striking statement but it rings true. Has teaching school children that the American founding was racist and evil improved race relations? Has it led to a more just nation? American education has shifted toward this negative, self-hating attitude most drastically over the last twenty years or so. Is the country less racist, or in any way improved, as a result? The fruits of this campaign of American self-hatred are not good. "It's about making us ashamed of where we came from. We, the people right in this room, have to fight against it."

There will be consequences from engaging in this fight for America—and so returns the reminder of the need for courage. It is not "just about social pressure." There is a clear message from the progressive elites that if Americans teach their children to "go astray of progressive orthodoxy, we're going to make you pay. We're going to punish you. We're going to hit you where it counts, which is in your wallet." The culture war comes with increasing threats of cancellation. If you voice the wrong opinion, you may lose your business contracts, your contacts, your professional license, and your job. This should be a sobering reflection for those who truly feel called to fight the political and cultural fights of our present day. It is quite difficult to be a warrior for the conservative cause without endangering one's livelihood. Vance was fortunate to work for men like Peter Thiel who supported his writing and his political endeavors. I personally went to work for a conservative Catholic nonprofit organization partly so I could continue on in my various political endeavors without fear that I would lose my ability to feed my family. Everyone's place in the fight will be different, but it is worth reflecting on the courage required and planning for the possible consequences of that courage.

After reflecting on the courage needed for the fight, Vance asks again who we are and what we are fighting for. Who are the Americans who continue to make up the patriotic population of this nation? The working class, who often lack a college education and who love our country, make up much of the patriotic population. They pay their taxes; they send their children into the military to fight America's wars. Vance notes that, if we are to support patriotism and a conservative politics that loves this nation, that means supporting this working-class base of citizens. The working-class base desperately needs help to continue to be patriotic, normal Americans because they are under attack and their situation is often precarious.

Those of us who live and work in the conservative intellectual upper-class are a bit more "cancel proof." We can shift jobs; we can work at aligned institutions and continue to support our families without the same fear of cancellation. But what about the working class? America's factory workers, bus drivers, and laborers cannot afford to be canceled, often not even for a day. And one wrong move can mean cancellation. If they use the wrong pronoun, publicly support the wrong candidate, or express certain opinions on social issues, it can mean the end of a career. These working-class Republicans need the conservative movement to have their backs; those of us who are "cancel-proof" need to speak up for these folks. "The culture war is a class war. It is a class war against the people that we represent and we defend, and that's why we've got to fight it."

Vance follows up this call to action with a warning about infighting within the conservative movement. Yes, those that make up the modern Right—Conservatives and Libertarians of various stripes—disagree strongly about important issues. These issues matter and need to be debated. But there is a danger of these debates becoming so definitive, so central in the minds of the conservative elite, that they end up fighting each other and becoming distracted from the greater fight against the Left for the soul of America.

How, then, do we win this fight? Vance claims that it starts by realizing how much we have lost within our major institutions: "we have lost every single major cultural institution in this country. Accept that. Think about it. Big finance, big tech, Wall Street, the biggest corporations, the universities, the media, and the government—there is not a single institution in this country that Conservatives currently control." This is a sobering and necessary thought to grapple with and accept. While Elon Musk's takeover of Twitter/X, the Trump victory in 2024, and a few other signs of hope are on the horizon, things are not good. The universities, major corporations, and government bureaucracies are not conservative institutions and it will be extremely difficult to reclaim them. Our best hope, Vance argues, is for Conservatives to control the American republic. Apple and Wall Street do not appear to be anywhere within the reach of Conservatives. But the American government is the one institution through which Conservatives may be able to gain serious institutional influence and control.

The argument to fight for institutional control is a powerful one. Libertarian theories of politics and government on the Right present a political problem. If Conservatives do not control any of our cultural institutions, there is simply nowhere else besides the government where the Right can exercise the influence necessary to combat the Leftist control that threatens to destroy this nation. If the only institution we can capture is the government, but then we have no political will to do anything but restrain government action when in office, there is little hope of conservative institutional reform in America. Conservatives "can't win anywhere else. This is a raw fact of cynical politics. If we're not willing to use the power given to us in the American constitutional republic, we are going to lose this country." This is why Vance, despite growing up and being formed in libertarian politics distrustful of government power, is open to conversations about using protective tariffs, regulating and reforming big tech, and breaking up corporate monopolies. If we don't consider these options, the ways in which conservative government can be used to make institutional improvements in America, then the right gives away its only opportunity to break the hold the left has on American institutions.

As Vance concludes this speech, he shifts his focus to one particular aspect of the modern Left that he believes needs to be addressed, even attacked: the culture of intentional childlessness. "I think the rejection of the American family is perhaps the most pernicious and most evil thing that the Left has done in this country." Vance takes aim at a number of particular rising stars in the Democrat party at the time—Kamala Harris, Pete Buttigieg, Cory Booker, Alexandria Ocasio Cortez—who come from very different backgrounds but (in 2021) were united by one single factor: none of them had any children. Vance asks something politically incorrect ("I'm going to get in trouble for this, but I want to ask the question anyway") but necessary here: Why is one of the two major political parties in the most powerful nation in the world controlled by people who have no children? This is not a matter of mere personal preference; intentional childlessness has serious consequences. Is it not disturbing that "the leaders of our country should be people who don't have a personal and direct stake in [the future] via their own offspring, via their own children and grandchildren?"

Of course, there are people who never meet the right person to marry and have children with. There are others who struggle with infertility. Vance is clear that these people suffer something outside of their control and they are clearly not the childless people he is talking about. But if our political elites, our media elites, and so many others who wield so much power for the future of our country are *intentionally choosing* not to have children, what does that say about their commitment to the future? Those who have intentionally chosen credentials, money, power, and worldly success at the expense of building a family that will outlive them for generations to come—aren't those people more likely to make decisions that do not prioritize the long-term good of our society and our nation? We need to ask this question because it is a novel situation: "It's never happened. This is a new thing in American life.... I think probably a new thing in world history."

It is worth pointing out that intentional childlessness is not only a novel thing; it is also a *bad* thing. Family life and children bring happiness. Further, it is the most natural way to live a human life. To intentionally forgo that is "not good. It's not healthy.... Kids are the ultimate way that we find self-meaning in life, whether your own children, your grandchildren, your nieces and nephews." This is not just a matter of demographic politics. Yes, Vance is adamant that we need more people and more babies, at least enough babies to sustain a population. But on a personal level, people who get married and have stable families that beget children are happy and they care about the world their children grow up in. Whether or not people make that choice for family, that self-sacrifice for a future that lives on after they are dead and gone, has political consequences for the way people will act. If we acknowledge that children and families are good, that they are necessary for a flourishing society, and that family formation makes people care about the long-term health of a society, it is prudent to question why we would elect leaders who intentionally avoid this family life. Is it wise to be led by people who choose not to have families, who do not have the bonds of children and grandchildren so naturally conducive to a love for society and a care for long-term societal health?

Vance states the principle—that children are good, that we need more children, and that more people should be forming families and having children—and then follows up with the idea that the government should enact policies that promote such a necessary societal good. Should the government follow the example of Hungary, giving tax credits and forgivable loans to married couples that stay together and have children? One can debate whether these policies will work and actually increase the number of stable families and children. But if the situation is dire and America desperately needs to encourage family formation, we need to at least consider putting creative options on the table. "We should give resources to parents who are going to have kids. We should make it easier to raise American families. And we should send the signal to the culture that we are the pro-family party and we're going to back it up with real policy."

Vance is open to the policy debate on what government actions will actually produce more healthy American families—it is not clear what will work and what will not in the face of this unprecedented situation. But Conservatives should start from the principle "that more healthy American families is a good thing." From there, we can have a real conversation and actually try things to improve the situation for the American family. People who invest their time and resources in their children, often at the expense of their own professional and financial improvement, are giving a great gift to society. Those children will fight America's wars, power America's economy, and innovate in American businesses. That sacrifice and choice to have more children in America should be encouraged. If child tax credits, student loan forgiveness for mothers, or any other policy will help solve the family formation and "birth dearth" problem, we should be open to them. If Conservatives oppose such policies, it should not be because they are government interventions but only because we are convinced those policies will not accomplish the intended goal of more children and more families.

At this point in his speech, Vance notes that many on the Left want to lower the voting age and give the vote to minors. Vance agrees that children have no representation in our democracy, but poses a radical alternative: "let's give votes to all children in this country, but let's give control over those votes to the parents of those children." This statement created quite the stir when Vance said it, but is it really that crazy? If two people decide to make the incredible sacrifice of time, energy, and resources to have children and invest in the future, is it really crazy to give those people a say, on behalf of their children who they love and sacrifice for, about what that future looks like?

The point of these proposals—whether they are really on the table or politically far-fetched—is to radically reorient the conservative movement around the family. The very purpose of the conservative movement, whatever the policy issue, is to make a good life and a good future for the American worker and the American family. Vance asks American Conservatives to have the courage to think and speak outside the box in trying to make this reorientation a reality. If we are so devoted to free market orthodoxy that we are not willing to enact policies that would increase family formation because the policies would involve government expenditures, we should be questioning whether our conservatism has become obsessed with the means and forgotten the ends for which we fight.

Vance ends with an anecdote about a woman from Ohio that he met. She is raising her grandchild because her daughter died of a heroin overdose. That woman cares deeply about the future because she cares about her grandbaby. And her number one political issue is immigration. Her focus on this issue has nothing to do with racism. It is about the drug that killed her daughter. This woman knows that an open southern border is flooding the country with deadly drugs that are killing our people and our future. The message is powerful: Conservatives need to reframe policy issues around the good of the family and the future of society. These issues are not about race, not about abstract economic or political theories. They are about the lives of real people. We need to create these captivating narratives. We need to tell stories. We need to convince people that our policy positions make for a better future. Vance's focus on the family and the American worker is a powerful way of reframing conservative issues to speak to both the heart and the mind.

IX

A Pro-Life Messaging Problem

Vance's focus on building a pro-family Republican Party is laudable and much needed. There is, however, one issue where I (and many Conservatives) disagree with the stance Trump and Vance took during the 2024 election: support for in-vitro fertilization (IVF) and mifepristone (the abortion pill). This criticism needs to be highlighted in a book that is otherwise almost entirely one of praise and admiration for JD Vance. The criticism is important not to "balance" the book, but to point out an important opportunity that would solidify Vance's relationship with the pro-life, religious conservative faction of the Republican Party without sacrificing political prudence.

Donald Trump governed as a pro-life president during his first term. In particular, he appointed three justices to the US Supreme Court that were responsible for overturning *Roe* and *Casey* and eliminating the legal fiction that abortion is a constitutional right. There is no denying that the Trump presidency did more for the pro-life movement than any other Republican was able to accomplish since *Roe*. Yet it seems that Trump's relationship with the pro-life community has largely been a transactional one. He knows that social Conservatives are a key part of his base and he must give them enough to keep them voting for him and for the Republican Party. This speculation is supported by the fact that in the past Trump used to consider himself "very pro-choice,"[18] as well as by his recent backing off from the pro-life issue in his 2024 re-election campaign.[19]

After the Supreme Court issued the *Dobbs* opinion overruling *Roe* and *Casey*, pro-lifers came off like dogs who had finally caught the truck and had no idea what to do with it. Forty-nine years of nationwide legal abortion took its toll on the culture. Even in red states, pro-life amendments were losing referenda votes and the pro-life cause looked like a political liability. So Trump, ever the pragmatic and transactional politician, backed away from pro-life stances. His support for the abortion pill, early-stage abortions, and IVF, given his past beliefs and his political pragmatism, is quite unsurprising. Trump likely figured that he had done enough for pro-lifers, that they had no better electoral options, and that he could therefore campaign to the middle on abortion without losing the votes of social Conservatives.

---

[18] "Trump in 1999: 'I am Very Pro-Choice'" Meet the Press, 1999, https://www.nbcnews.com/meet-the-press/video/trump-in-1999-i-am-very-pro-choice-480297539914.

[19] Sarah McCammon, "Trump is Trying to Allay Concerns On Abortion, and Abortion Opponents Aren't Happy," *NPR*, August 26, 2024, https://www.npr.org/2024/08/26/nx-s1-5090224/trump-abortion-pills-comstock.

This political calculation and pivot on pro-life issues is one thing from President Trump. But Vance is a bit of a different case because he is, on principle, clearly a pro-life Catholic. Vance is not confused or ambivalent about the issue on a moral or philosophical level. In early 2022 he said he "certainly would like abortion to be illegal nationally."[20] He also expressed in 2021 an awareness that "two wrongs don't make a right," signaling that a woman being a victim of rape does not transform abortion from an immoral to a moral act.[21]

Additionally, in 2017 Vance wrote the introduction to a Heritage Foundation report that addressed a variety of cultural issues.[22] Part of that report opposed IVF as contributing to, rather than alleviating, the problem of infertility and low birth rates. To be clear, Vance's introduction did not make this argument about IVF, but the anti-IVF argument was made in a report that Vance put his name at the top of. At the very least, Vance has affiliated himself with the conservative Christian intellectual movement that understands the moral problem with supporting anti-life practices like abortion or IVF in any way.

The IVF issue contains two distinct moral issues that should be separated and explained. First, there is the problem of "playing God," of removing the creation of human life from its natural process within the sexual act. Every human being, by nature, should be conceived by the sexual act between a man and a

---

[20] Andrew Kaczynski and Em Steck, "JD Vance said in 2022 he 'would like abortion to be illegal nationally,'" *CNN*, July 17, 2024, https://www.cnn.com/2024/07/17/politics/kfile-jd-vance-abortion-comments/index.html.

[21] Nathaniel Weixel, "JD Vance's views on healthcare: What to know," *The Hill*, July 16, 2024, https://thehill.com/policy/healthcare/4775098-vance-healthcare-positions/.

[22] "2017 Index of Culture and Opportunity," *The Heritage Foundation*, https://www.heritage.org/2017-index-culture-and-opportunity.

woman, giving each child a natural mother and father. Any other method of creating human life is unnatural and likely carries with it a host of unprecedented and unintended consequences.

Second, there is a separate pro-life problem that many people still do not fully realize. For every embryo conceived and implanted through IVF, many more embryos are generally created and then either discarded or frozen for potential later implantation. For anyone sympathetic to the pro-life argument, this means that IVF has led to millions of human beings being either killed or frozen when they are not selected for implantation. Thus, anyone opposed to abortion on principle cannot support IVF as it is currently practiced.

The early pro-life stances and associations of JD Vance show that he has a clear understanding of the fundamental basis for being pro-life. A child in the womb is a human being from the moment of conception. The circumstances surrounding conception and pregnancy can never make an abortion morally acceptable, because it is always the intentional killing of an innocent human being. Therefore, a principled pro-lifer is always pro-life because killing an innocent human being is always gravely wrong.

Yet Vance has clearly attempted to moderate his stance on abortion in recent years, at least for campaign purposes. In July 2024, just days before Vance was publicly announced as Trump's running mate, Vance appeared on *Meet the Press* and agreed that he supports the abortion drug "mifepristone being available."[23] Also, when asked about IVF, Vance said to a radio station during the 2024 presidential campaign that he and Trump and "pretty

---

[23] Kristen Welker, "Meet the Press—July 7, 2024," *NBC News*, July 7, 2024, https://www.nbcnews.com/meet-the-press/meet-press-july-7-2024-n1310187.

JD VANCE AND THE FUTURE OF THE REPUBLICAN PARTY

much every Republican that I know is pro-fertility treatments." This is a bit of a hedge. There are plenty of "fertility treatments" that are good, acceptable, moral practices and have nothing to do with IVF. Vance didn't explicitly say he supports IVF in this statement. But the fact remains that, in the last couple years, Vance has intentionally toned down his pro-life rhetoric.

Vance is ideologically pro-life and heavily influenced by Catholic social teaching in the way he views human life, procreation, sex, and so on. But he has also clearly moderated his political stances on these controversial life issues—likely in an attempt to keep his political stances within the realm of what is possible in the current political climate.

There are two distinct points to be made about the proper stance pro-lifers within the Republican Party ought to adopt in our increasingly secular political culture. The first is a criticism addressed to the pro-life social conservative community, the second a criticism of Vance and many other Republicans attempting to moderate on the abortion and IVF issues.

The Pro-Life Movement Must Learn Incrementalism in the Face of Reality

Pro-life Conservatives need to face a hard but obvious truth. The political community in the United States is not pro-life. Democrats have supported abortion rights as a party platform and almost no dissenters remain. There are very few pro-life Democrats left in national politics. And while the Republican Party has long been the party that has opposed legal abortion, a Pew Research poll in 2022 showed that 38 percent *of Republicans* believe abortion should be legal in most/all cases.[24] This statistic reveals a problem. There is no practical way for the Republican Party to promote a platform that includes banning abortion in all cases without exception (including pregnancy resulting from rape, early-stage abortion via the abortion pill, and the disposing of un-implanted embryos during the IVF process). Yes, this is the consistent, principled pro-life stance. But sadly (and obviously), there is simply no electoral majority in favor of such positions right now.

Now that *Roe v. Wade* has been overruled, there is little more that can be done politically to restrict abortion (especially at the federal level) until pro-life activists and educators transform the culture by convincing more Americans to fully embrace the pro-life, anti-abortion position. Until then, it is reasonable for pro-life Conservatives to be politically prudent and choose not to promote policies that would ban mifepristone or IVF. This is a hard pill to swallow for pro-lifers, because every abortion means the death of an innocent child created in the image and likeness of God. I am one of those pro-lifers, and I share in the disgust that we cannot completely ban this barbaric practice in America today. But we cannot. Sadly, the only result of an aggressive push to ban all instances of abortion in the current political climate would be political defeat.

Vance realized this unfortunate political reality in 2023, after the successful referendum in Ohio to enshrine abortion as a right in the state constitution. Ohio is a reliably Republican state at this point. Trump defeated Biden by eight points in Ohio in

---

[24] Michael Lipka, "A closer look at Republicans who favor legal abortion and Democrats who oppose it," *Pew Research Center*, June 17, 2022, https://www.pewresearch.org/short-reads/2022/06/17/a-closer-look-at-republicans-who-favor-legal-abortion-and-democrats-who-oppose-it/.

JD VANCE AND THE FUTURE OF THE REPUBLICAN PARTY

2020. He also defeated Kamala Harris by eleven points in 2024. In the wake of that tragic defeat, Vance called the result a "gut punch" that made him realize how little voters trust Republicans on the issue of life, pregnancy, and abortion.[25] This was a turning point where Vance began to see the abortion issue as something on which pro-lifers need to make cultural changes before further political changes are possible. Again, many pro-lifers may not like this. But after watching pro-life referenda fail in several red states in the years after the *Dobbs* decision, hesitation and moderation on the issue is a reasonable and moral political position for a pro-life Christian to take in the current climate. The decision that further political action on abortion, in the current political climate, is unlikely to save lives and is likely to cause electoral problems can be a matter of prudence rather than cowardice.

The Problem of Active Support

When Vance chose to go along with the Republican Party platform and moderate on the pro-life issue, he was—from a Christian perspective—*almost* correct in the way he went about it. There is nothing contrary to the Catholic faith about admitting that there is no political appetite for a ban on abortion or IVF in America. But as a Catholic and a Christian, Vance, along with all Christian politicians, has a moral duty not to *support* what is objectively a grave evil. The word "support" may seem to be a subtle or trivial issue, but it is not.

It would be fine, even prudent, for Vance and the GOP to state their message in words like this: "The reality is that the

---

[25] Elizabeth Crisp, "JD Vance: Ohio's abortion vote 'was a gut punch,'" *The Hill*, November 8, 2023, https://thehill.com/homenews/senate/4300013-jd-vance-ohio-abortion-vote/.

culture in America is not fundamentally pro-life. While there are some things we can do to improve the culture of life, there is no political appetite to ban the abortion pill or IVF in America until there is a dramatic cultural change. I believe, by scientific evidence, by my faith, and by my understanding of the law, that all unborn children are human beings entitled to legal protection. Therefore, I believe all abortions are wrong. While I pray for a political culture where this is possible, we are not there. While I will work to save as many innocent human lives as politically possible, our administration is not going to act—in fact, it cannot act—on these issues."

Such messaging would accomplish two goals: it would use the "bully pulpit" to explain that abortion is always a grave evil—even in the first trimester, via the abortion pill, or through IVF (after all: a person is a person, no matter how small),[26] and it would avoid attempting to legislate on an issue where there is currently no political appetite for change. It is okay to choose not to legislate on an issue; it is quite another to offer active support on an issue that is gravely immoral. I hope and pray that Vance and the Republican Party can find a way to be politically prudent, which in the current climate probably means openly refusing to legislate on these pro-life issues while finding ways to speak against them and refusing to actively support them.

Finding a Delicate Balance

The Trump/Vance Republican Party needs to be careful not to support immoral actions. Further, it is objectively a scandal for a Catholic politician to say he supports access to immoral

---

[26] Dr. Seuss, *Horton Hears a Who!* (Random House, 1954).

procedures like the abortion pill. I hope and pray that the Vance team will take this distinction to heart, so that he can continue to exercise political prudence on the abortion issue without indicating active support for something that is evil.

But Vance is also onto something important, something that many pro-life Christians have failed to accept and acknowledge. Vance rightly explained in the *New York Post* in 2024 that "Catholic social teaching is obviously very robust. I think that no person who, or at least no one I know who's Catholic, doesn't accept that just because the Catholic Church teaches something, doesn't mean you necessarily as a legislator need to affect that to public policy."[27] And he is quite right about that. While there are some things—like abortion—that are always objectively wrong and that cannot be supported by Catholic politicians, there are limits to what can be achieved politically on these moral issues.

America is not a Catholic, nor currently even a particularly Christian, republic. This is simply reality. Unless and until the nation's voters return to a faith-based view of life and sexuality, there is little to no ability for conservative Catholics to impose Catholic social teaching as the policy of the United States government. It is neither necessary nor feasible for American Catholics to try to do so.

Republicans (especially faithful Christians) can never actively support evil actions. But in the reality of our modern, secular culture, it is also imprudent and politically impossible to aggressively attempt to ban the abortion pill or IVF. The only result

---

[27] Diana Nerozzi, "JD Vance explains how his Catholic faith aligns with IVF, abortion policies: 'Accept that you live in a Democratic society,'" *New York Post,* August 15, 2024, https://nypost.com/2024/08/15/us-news/jd-vance-explains-how-his-catholic-faith-aligns-with-policies-on-abortion-ivf-you-have-to-accept-that-you-live-in-a-democratic-society/.

will be political loss; no lives will be saved in the process. As this reality becomes clear to more Conservatives, hopefully the Republican Party can do a better job of learning how to message and use the bully pulpit to speak a pro-life message while acknowledging the limits of what can be done politically on the life issue. And Vance, an intelligent, well-spoken, and Catholic Republican leader, should be at the forefront of learning how to prudently message and govern on this difficult issue.

X

Vance the Politician

The previous chapters have examined JD Vance's biography, his political philosophy and policy priorities, and his view of the proper role of government. But a complete profile of a politician needs to focus not just on his thought but on the practical political skills of the man. While common usage tends to refer to someone as a "politician" in a negative sense, political skills are good and necessary for Conservatives to succeed in politics. The smartest conservative intellectuals and policy professionals cannot do much good if they do not understand how to win campaigns, message and speak to voters, build coalitions, make deals, and agree on compromises. So while Vance's philosophies and ideas are central to this book, it is time to look at his practical skills as a politician. This will both shed light on how Vance has risen to his current position and on how he can make valuable contributions to the success of President Trump's second term and to the Republican Party moving forward.

The Vance Orbit: Donors, Intellectuals, Political Operatives

Before talking about Vance's political strategy as well as many of the bills he has sponsored, it is worth taking a look at some of the political characters with whom Vance has surrounded himself. The conservative movement is an eclectic mix of nationalists, populists, religious Conservatives, classical Liberals, post-Liberals, and others. The analysis of Vance's various political and intellectual affiliations does not allow a simple identification of the "type" of Conservative, the subset within the movement, that explains JD Vance. Vance is deeply familiar with all of these movements, and he is influenced by several of them. Vance serves as a great example of how to understand and unite the various ideologies within the Republican Party, overcome the intra-party squabbles, and take action.

JD Vance has more than a passing acquaintance with the Silicon Valley tech elite, many of whom are quite wealthy and lean more Libertarian than Conservative. Vance began his career in Silicon Valley in venture capital. He worked closely with Peter Thiel. He received money for his own venture capital firm from big, wealthy names like Thiel and Marc Andreessen. Some social Conservatives are understandably wary of Vance's ties to the Silicon Valley elite. After all, many of these people—Andreessen is an obvious example—are admittedly Liberals. Andreessen supported Democrats until very recently, when he realized the Democrat party had veered too far Left and was threatening to completely stifle business and innovation and destroy the country. Conservatives are justifiably concerned that an alliance with center-left Liberals/Libertarians from places like Silicon Valley threatens to transform the Republican Party from a conservative party to a moderate one.

Yes, Vance worked in Silicon Valley. Many of these venture capitalists are Vance's personal friends and mentors. One can have friends and still be one's own man. People like Peter Thiel have seen that Vance is a brilliant, talented man who can do much good as a public figure in this country. But that does not mean Thiel or anyone else has political or ideological influence over Vance's politics. It is quite possible—indeed rather probable—that Vance has simply befriended and impressed these people enough that they have backed him for political office even if they don't see eye to eye on their vision of politics and government.

Politics is about building coalitions to deal with the political reality of a particular time and place. Two things have become obvious in American politics in recent years: social Conservatives are not a majority and the Democrat Party has moved so far to the Left that it has alienated many moderates and Liberals who were formerly part of its base. With these realities in mind, building coalitions with demographics that have not been part of the Republican Party in decades past—including libertarian-leaning tech bros and venture capitalists—is really not optional. Yes, Conservatives need to be aware that they are forming alliances with groups that have seriously different worldviews and policy preferences on certain issues. Coalitions are often in tension. But that is how politics works. So Conservatives who may be uncomfortable with the new allies who have come into the Republican Party from the Left—from Elon Musk and Mark Andreessen to Tulsi Gabbard and RFK Jr.—are right to be wary but also need to remember that political parties cannot be gatekeepers for ideological purity and also win elections.

Vance has interesting friends in the world of Silicon Valley tech bros, but that is not the only connection worth mentioning. Vance has deep ties to the conservative intellectual movement. He is not simply a politician who has given speeches or interviews at some of the premier American conservative think tanks; he has really been a part of these intellectual circles. Vance has been a great supporter and friend of the Claremont Institute, a conservative think tank whose mission is to teach the principles of the American founding to modern leaders and statesmen. Vance publicly praised Claremont for the contributions of its work to the good of America and particularly to Vance's work as a US Senator: "The [Claremont Institute's] Center for the American Way of Life is doing incredible work to restore the American system. Their analysis and acumen have been invaluable for my work in the United States Senate."[28] Vance has written for elite conservative religious magazines such as *First Things* and the *Lamp*. He has been closely affiliated with groups like National Conservatism, where he gave his now-famous speech "America is a Nation" in 2024. Vance has surrounded himself and been affiliated with some of the brightest and most interesting minds in the conservative intellectual movement today. It is encouraging that such a powerful and successful Republican politician takes the intellectual life seriously.

---

[28] "Claremont Goes to Washington," *Claremont Institute*, July 19, 2024, https://www.claremont.org/claremont-goes-to-washington/.

Political Operatives

While observers like to focus on the big donors and influential figures that a politician surrounds himself with, there is another class of people within the circle of a politician that can be easily overlooked but whose presence matters greatly: political operatives. The people who work behind the scenes on a politician's campaigns and on his government staff say a lot about the kind of politician he is. While Vance has surrounded himself with more individuals than can be named and analyzed here, a couple things are worth noting.

First, Vance has kept a loyal and consistent inner circle in the years since he got involved in politics.[29] His long-time friend and advisor, Jai Chabria, remains one of the vice president's closest senior advisors. In fact, many of Vance's original advisors from the beginnings of his campaign for the Senate remain within his inner circle. This alone says a lot about Vance's consistency. Vance is less likely than many politicians to change his stances and his priorities as he rises in political life, because he is keeping the same inner circle around him. Personnel is policy, as they say. So the fact that Vance has largely kept the same personnel over the years sends a signal that he is likely to remain consistent in the way he campaigns and governs. Vance's political past will tell us a lot about his political future.

Second, Vance is ahead of the curve. Anyone familiar with the world of insider politics knows there is a major problem with the political consulting class. Many of the highly paid political

---

[29] Henry J. Gomez, "Complete synergy and trust': Vance staffs VP's office with allies — and no objections from Trump," *NBC News*, January 30, 2025, https://www.nbcnews.com/politics/donald-trump/vance-staffs-vp-office-allies-no-trump-objections-rcna189472.

consultants running campaigns and administrations have been doing this for decades—or were taught and influenced by those who have been doing this for decades. The result is an inability to realize how much the modern world of smartphones, social media, streaming services, and the corresponding short attention spans of voters has changed the way campaigns must be run. What issues to focus on, how to message, and where precious campaign dollars should be spent are all questions that require entirely different answers today than they did a decade or two ago.

Vance is an example of a savvy modern politician who understands the changing realities of politics. A prime example is Luke Thompson's work on Vance's US Senate campaign.[30] Early on in the primary, Peter Thiel donated several million dollars to a Super PAC backing Vance. Luke Thompson, a brilliant political strategist, knew that Vance was a new political candidate who would be fighting an uphill battle in a crowded primary. When the Super PAC was suddenly well-funded with Thiel's money, Thompson was the visionary who spent that money in a way that could win the race. But Super PACs, unlike campaigns, can receive unlimited amounts of money from a single donor and are strictly forbidden from communicating directly with the campaign. So Luke Thompson, a trusted Vance advisor, went to work for the Super PAC and was not allowed to coordinate with the Vance campaign.

Thompson's operation spent the money primarily on gathering data rather than on traditional campaigning. Thompson assembled information based on opposition research and extensive

---

[30] Connor Perrett, "GOP super PAC built a secret but public website to funnel information to JD Vance and skirt federal laws, Politico reports," *Business Insider*, May 4, 2022, https://www.businessinsider.com/super-pac-secret-public-website-info-to-vance-politico-2022-5.

JD VANCE AND THE FUTURE OF THE REPUBLICAN PARTY

polling. He dug into Vance's potential strengths and weaknesses, his primary opponents, the most effective ways to frame Vance's political messages, and strategic tactics on how to court Donald Trump's endorsement in the primary. This was valuable information, but there was a problem. Thompson could no longer coordinate or communicate privately with Vance and his campaign.

So Thompson took a brilliant risk. He uploaded all the information he was gathering onto a public website. This meant that Vance's opponents and members of the public could see the website. But by building the site with the right keywords, messaging, and so on, Thompson gambled on the fact that Vance's campaign would find the site, understand where the information was coming from, and be able to use it without violating the law by directly coordinating with the Super PAC. The gamble paid off. Thompson's cutting-edge tactics gave Vance the research and data he needed to win an incredibly competitive primary, thus going from a political unknown to a rising star in the American political world.

This example shows an unusual political vision. Unfortunately, most Republican political candidates continue to spend money in the conventional way, buying campaign signs and television ads, avoiding controversial issues, and campaigning as if we still live in the political world of the 1990s. Vance understands tech and the realities of modern society. He knows that he needs to surround himself with strategists and thinkers who are adapting to modern circumstances. Not only does that display Vance's insight and intelligence, it shows that he knows what it takes to win competitive campaigns in the twenty-first century.

Practical Politics: How to Win Elections

Politics is shifting in the modern era. There is a realignment within the Republican Party, which will force party leaders to either acknowledge the reality of their new working-class base or fade into irrelevance. Modern technology has completely transformed the way campaigns need to be run and campaign dollars need to be spent. Politicians need to adapt, but they need to be aware of which variables actually make the difference.

The 2022 midterm elections were hopeful for Republicans. Then the results came in. The anticipated red wave was a red trickle and the election did not bring in strong Republican majorities. As hope quickly changed to disappointment, the various Republican factions, consultants, and political operatives moved swiftly from taking credit to passing blame. Vance wrote a post-mortem on the less-than-impressive Republican electoral results in a piece titled *Don't Blame Trump*[31] at The American Conservative.

Vance begins the piece by noting that, once the 2022 midterm results came in and were less than impressive, the most common response was for Republicans to blame Donald Trump. Trump-aligned candidates lost close races. Trump was blamed for dragging the party down despite the fact that he was not on the ticket. Vance begins, not by addressing the Trump factor, but by pointing to a clear and important problem Republicans need to address in the coming years: "any effort to blame Trump—or [Senate Majority Leader Mitch] McConnell for that matter—ignores a major structural advantage for Democrats: money. Money is how candidates fund the all-important advertising

---

[31] Sen. J.D. Vance, "Don't Blame Trump," *The American Conservative*, November 14, 2022, https://www.theamericanconservative.com/dont-blame-trump/.

that reaches swing voters, and it's how candidates fund turnout operations." While strategists and political pundits wanted an easy scapegoat—blame Trump, or the abortion issue, or any particular matter of messaging or strategy—it is worth pausing and making sure we are not focusing on minutiae and missing the big picture. Money wins elections.

While Republicans overpay legacy-style consultants to generate lists of potential donors, Democrats have been working through a national platform called ActBlue, which funnels small dollar donations from Democrats all over the country into winnable elections. Vance notes that Republicans have tried to close the gap with donations through Super PACs, but this causes a spending gap because political campaigns are treated differently than typical for-profit organizations, campaigns pay way less for advertising than PACs. Therefore, money from small-dollar donations given directly to campaigns goes a lot further than money given to PACs. This puts the Republicans far behind in campaign spending.

Vance uses the money problem to put the 2022 midterms in perspective. When reviewing non-incumbent Republicans who lost races throughout the country, both Trump-aligned and anti-Trump Republican candidates were outspent and lost. The main issue (likely related to the money problem) is that the Republican working-class base does not turn out in high numbers during midterm elections. Add the fact that Democrats were much better at using early voting (both in-person and by mail), and the Republicans had a major problem that had almost everything to do with money and get-out-the-vote operations, and very little to do with particular candidates or messaging. Vance implores party leadership to stop blaming Trump or MAGA and to start addressing the real problems: "Any autopsy of Republican underperformance ought to focus on how to close the national money gap, and how to turn out less engaged Republicans during midterm elections. These are the problems we have, and rather than blaming everyone else, it's time for party leaders to admit we have these problems and work to solve them."

This matters not just as a diagnostic to improve the Republican Party in the future, but to show Vance's solid political insight. Vance wrote this piece in late 2022; it appears prophetic after the 2024 presidential election. In 2024, public figures from Scott Presler to Charlie Kirk mobilized massive efforts to register voters, win swing states, and get voters to turn out and vote. The Republicans effectively closed the early voting gap and got their voters to vote by mail in sufficient numbers to neutralize the Democrat early voting advantage. The fundraising gap was lessened due to Republicans aggressively raising small dollar donations via text and email campaigns. The result speaks for itself: despite his bold MAGA campaign (including the selection of JD Vance rather than a moderate VP to "balance the ticket"), Trump won big. He won all seven swing states, Republicans took both houses of Congress, and a Republican presidential candidate won the popular vote for the first time in twenty years. Money and voter turnout, rather than abandoning the MAGA platform or downplaying controversial policy issues, won the election. Vance's political instincts were right on: fix the money problem and the voter turnout problem, and Republicans will win.

Vance the Tactical Politician

In early 2024, Vance wrote an essay at The American Conservative titled *The Republican Plot Against Donald Trump*.[32] For those who don't recall, there was a political fight over an attempt to create a bipartisan border security bill and to condition any further aid for Ukraine on the passage of the border bill. The short version of the story is that a bipartisan border security package was negotiated, but it was unacceptable to many Republicans (and was likely unnecessary because there are already adequate laws on the books to secure the border that simply need to be enforced). Donald Trump was among those who spoke out against the border deal, making clear his position that the problem at the border did not require a bill but only competent action by President Biden, who already had the legal and financial resources he needed. The problem was not law or resources, but the will to secure the border.

As it became clear that the border security part of the bill was dead on arrival in Congress, the Ukraine aid continued. Despite the desire of a growing number of Republicans to close the spigot of funds flowing from the American taxpayer to the Ukraine war, there were enough hawkish Republicans focused on Ukraine-spending to work with the Democrats and keep the money flowing, even after the border security part of the deal fell apart.

This episode may seem like a typical, dated political fight without too much long-term significance. But the way that it

---

[32] Sen. J.D. Vance, "The Republican Plot Against Donald Trump," *The American Conservative*, February 12, 2024, https://www.theamericanconservative.com/how-congress-is-pursuing-endless-war-in-ukraine-and-trying-to-stop-a-trump-election/.

played out, and particularly JD Vance's analysis of the situation, reveal two important aspects of Vance's political skills. First, Vance made clear the need for Republicans to prioritize foreign policy in one's backyard (the Mexican border) rather than overseas excursions that are not in the American interest (endless funding of Ukraine). Second, Vance makes a strong argument about how political trade-offs are supposed to work and how Republicans risk snatching "defeat from the jaws of victory" through political mismanagement. Politics has important consequences, but there are also aspects of politics that are a game of strategy. Republicans need to play it well if they are to wield power and effect change.

Vance understands the realities of political maneuvering. His account of this political fight reveals his practical understanding of the compromises necessary in politics. It is easy for politicians, especially those running major national campaigns, to adopt a strong posture on issues that are popular with their base, even when those issues are not politically viable and those positions will never become law. Vance has a keen sense of what is politically possible and does not want ideals to prevent practical political improvements. During this fight in 2024, Vance applied the logic of the politically possible to the continued funding of the Ukraine war. Despite being one of the most consistently skeptical senators regarding Ukraine aid from the beginning, Vance knew that there were enough pro-Ukraine Republicans in the Senate to make it nearly impossible to fully cut off aid. He also knew that an unsecure southern border is an existential threat and that Ukraine might be the carrot and stick needed to actually make improvements to border security.

So despite Vance's strong disagreement with American funding of the war in Ukraine, he and many of his Republican colleagues saw—at least at the beginning of the negotiations, before the ultimately inadequate and unhelpful bipartisan deal was negotiated—an opportunity for real progress on the southern border: "We argued that we could condition further Ukraine aid on decreased illegal border crossings. In other words, Congress would appropriate money to Ukraine in stages: if Biden refused to drive down border crossings, he wouldn't get his money for Ukraine." This type of tradeoff is a smart political exchange, where factions each get something they want. But many idealists and political observers don't seem to understand the necessity of such deals. The reality is that, in 2024, nearly all Democrats and many Republicans in both houses of Congress were in favor of at least some support to the Ukrainian war effort. Despite Vance's principled stance on stopping US funding of this war, he knew there was no political appetite to cease aid to Ukraine all together. But if the aid was inevitably going to continue—which it was in early 2024—it was a smart move to try to tie the Ukraine funding to a useful conservative goal, such as limiting the number of illegal border crossings. If you can't get the best result on one area of policy, it is okay (and indeed, often politically expedient) to make a compromise on that area in order to get a better result on another policy issue. Vance's analysis of how this situation went down is a reminder that Republicans need to be better at getting the best possible deal done, rather than dying on the hill of an impossible and idealistic best-case scenario for no practical benefit.

Republicans, encouraged by Senator McConnell, opted to negotiate a bipartisan border security bill that they knew would be opposed by Trump and his allies on the immigration crisis. Critics saw the proposal as a gift to the Democrats during an election cycle where the border was a hot topic. Why make it look like the Democrats were taking action on the border (something they failed to do for years) during an election? That bill was always going to be dead on arrival, which allowed McConnell and his allies to praise the bipartisan effort to secure the border and blame the MAGA wing for killing it, knowing that it never had a chance to pass. Then they could say they tried on the whole border security thing and go back to their true priority: funding Ukraine.

The takeaway is that Republicans have severely divergent priorities and this is a grave problem for the Republican legislative agenda. During this particular conflict, there were many Republicans strongly in favor of continued funding to Ukraine, while "a majority of House Republicans oppose[d] further Ukraine aid, and demand strong border security measures regardless of the details of a Ukraine package." Therefore, Ukraine aid appropriations might have easily passed the Senate but would likely have endangered the Republican Speaker's position if he introduced them on the House floor. This tension was especially present in the new Congress beginning in 2025, where the Republican majority in the House was even slimmer than in the previous Congress. When Republicans control the 435 member House of Representatives by literally a couple of votes, introducing a bill that flies in the face of the priorities of many House Republicans threatens to break the Republican majority and prevent them from acting as a united front capable of passing any useful legislation.

These types of situations create real problems for Republicans' ability to govern. If establishment Republicans and Democrats agree on policy issues like Ukraine funding, then establishment Republicans, especially in the Senate, can feed the media narrative that it is Trump and the "MAGA Republicans," rather than the will of a majority of Americans, that is creating the dysfunction and chaos in Congress. The establishment wing of the party, particularly with its foreign policy desires and loose spending habits, is undermining some of the most important priorities of the Republican base and the American people.

It will take more than conservative policy ideas and courage for Republicans on the "new Right" to win elections and govern effectively. Yes, we need rock-ribbed Conservatives who love America to occupy political office. But we also need leaders with the political intuition and strategic thinking to navigate these complex intra-party issues. Vance has identified a grave problem within the party, particularly in the Senate. Those who are united within the Republican Party have vastly different policy priorities and it is not easy to get these factions to come together, even on important votes.

Seeing the problem is necessary in order to do something about it. Vance is a leader who sees all the moving parts within the Republican Party and the different branches of government, one who can determine what is an impossible ideal and what is actually possible. Vance brings hope, the hope that Republicans can elevate talented political leaders who are able to maneuver through the different interests and factions in the party and actually implement America first policies. If Republicans elect staunch Conservatives who don't know how to play the game of compromise and political maneuvering, all the pure ideals and good will in the world will not translate to policy wins. Vance is a political strategist who knows not just what goals need to be implemented, but the game that needs to be played and won to enact those policy goals.

XI

Vance the Legislator

Writers, political pundits, and intellectuals can talk quite a bit about policy priorities, about what laws should be introduced and focused on by lawmakers. While speeches and op-eds may really tell you something about how a politician thinks about policy and how he will govern, there is no substitute for the actual legislative record of someone who has served in the legislature. While Vance spent only two years in the US Senate, he was an active and vocal senator who was primary sponsor of dozens of bills in the Senate.[33] By focusing on some of the more important bills that Vance was willing to put his name on as sponsor, we can get a glimpse into his policy priorities in a way that goes beyond the study of essays and speeches.

---

[33] "118th Congress Bills Sponsored by JD Vance," *Open Secrets*, https://www.opensecrets.org/members-of-congress/j-d-vance/bills?cid=N00048832&cycle=2024&spon_type=sponsor.

Before digging into a few of the particular bills Vance sponsored in the Senate, a caveat is appropriate. Yes, putting one's name on a bill as a sponsor signals that the legislator prioritizes the legislation and is willing to be closely associated with the bill. But the act of sponsoring or voting for a bill does not necessarily mean the legislator cares deeply about passing that particular law. Some bills are introduced to make a point even though they have no chance of passing. Others are introduced, not to become law, but to put legislators on the record to publicly reveal which side of a debate they fall on. Finally, remember that the Democrats had control of the Senate during the two years Vance was a senator. Therefore, most bills sponsored and introduced by Republicans in 2023–2024 were unlikely to be enacted into law.

In short, the bills Vance sponsored in the Senate give us a glimpse into his legislative priorities, but motives can be complex and it is up to the reader to weigh for himself the significance of these sponsored bills.

English Language Unity Act

The first bill Vance sponsored as a senator was the English Language Unity Act of 2023.[34] The bill, like most bills Vance sponsored while Republicans were in the minority in the Senate, was sent to committee but never passed into law. The effect of this law would have been to declare English as the official language of the United States, which it currently is not. This is not mere symbolism. The bill recognizes the significance of language to unify a diverse people:

---

[34] English Language Unity Act of 2023, S. 1109, 118th Cong. (2023), https://www.govinfo.gov/content/pkg/BILLS-118s1109is/html/BILLS-118s1109is.htm.

1. The United States is comprised of individuals from diverse ethnic, cultural, and linguistic backgrounds.
2. Throughout the history of the United States, a common thread binding citizens of differing backgrounds has been the English language.

As Vance has frequently pointed out, America is suffering from a lack of patriotism and national identity. Americans are being taught, through schools, universities, and media outlets, to hate their own country and heritage. America has always been a diverse nation of people from different ethnic backgrounds, religions, and cultures. But there used to be a notion of a "melting pot," of a process by which people from various nations and cultures come here and *become American.*

As this unifying American identity has faded, as a common love for the origins, the story, and the Constitution of the United States has ceased to be a unifying bond for Americans, Vance introduced this bill to propose the beginnings of a solution. It is not acceptable for people to come to America and live in America without adopting common customs, beliefs, and traditions that unite them as Americans.

America is unique. Unlike England, France, Italy, or most countries around the world, there is not really an American ethnicity. While most early Americans were Anglo-Saxon Protestants, few today maintain that an English background is what makes one American. Americans are united by a cultural process of becoming part of the American people, not by a common *ethnic* heritage. While people over the years have referred to America as an "idea" rather than a normal nation, Vance has vocally and repeatedly disagreed with that, including in his speech at the 2024 Republican National Convention: "America is not just an idea. It is a group of people with a shared history and a common future."³⁵ Yes, America is uniquely grounded in the ideas of its founding, the ideals found in the Declaration of Independence and the Constitution. But as Vance has said, America is not, it cannot be, only an idea. If all it takes to be an American is a love of the American idea, that is not sufficient to create a nation. People have to live here, on American soil, sharing American history and shared traditions, in order to be part of a nation.

While this is all heady, high-level stuff, the ideal of reunifying Americans around a shared history and a common culture needs to start somewhere. Vance's proposal to unite Americans around the English language as the official language of the nation is a modest but useful place to start. In order for the American people to be united around a shared history and a common culture, sharing a common language is a prerequisite. This should not be controversial. People from diverse cultures are free to keep their customs, their traditions, and even their languages. But American history, law, literature, and everything that creates a shared American culture is written in English. Sharing a common language is more than a symbol of unity; it is a literal necessity to have a united people. And while this may appear to be a symbolic bill (since English is de facto the national language), declaring an official language could have important effects as an increasingly diverse American population has led to a loss of the universal use of English. Citizens concerned with public schools teaching in Spanish or even Arabic may want to take this proposal seriously.

---

[35] Fred Bauer, "America Beyond Ideas," *National Review*, July 25, 2024, https://www.nationalreview.com/corner/america-beyond-ideas/.

Financial Regulatory Accountability Act of 2023

Another bill introduced by Vance early in his Senate career was the Financial Regulatory Accountability Act,[36] which intended to establish an office of inspector general to investigate instances of abuse and misconduct committed by regulatory agencies. The goal was to allow regulated entities (such as businesses in the finance and banking industries) to report misconduct by the agencies that oversee and regulate them.

The creation of a government office that would monitor abuse by regulatory agencies serves a couple useful purposes. First, pro-business Republicans who worry that overregulation is a serious problem that stifles success and creativity in American companies would appreciate such accountability. It sends a clear message. Regulatory agencies are limited by the law and must be reined in so they are not free to abuse and harass regulated companies with inappropriate and excessive investigations and regulatory actions. Someone has to regulate the regulators or they can easily get out of control.

Second, there is a legitimate fear that regulatory agencies are not even-handed. Just as the IRS has a lot of power and discretion to target and audit individuals and organizations, so too do the regulatory agencies that oversee the finance and banking industry. In a nation committed to impartial justice and the rule of law, people and businesses should not have to fear that they will be singled out and targeted for audits or regulatory investigations because of their political views, religious affiliations, or any other viewpoint-based reason. Having an inspector general oversee

---

[36] Financial Regulatory Accountability Act of 2023, S. 2335, 118th Cong. (2023), https://www.congress.gov/bill/118th-congress/senate-bill/2335/text.

these regulatory agencies would be a useful check to ensure that investigation and enforcement actions are even-handed and do not display trends of targeting individuals or entities with particular viewpoints. If organizations are being targeted, they should have some recourse: an office tasked with tracking instances of unfair investigation or enforcement. Both conservative activists involved in controversial work and those who are simply concerned with burdensome overregulation should welcome oversight of these powerful regulatory agencies.

A Bill to Restrict the Chinese Government

As noted earlier, Vance has a clear vision about US foreign policy. While there are many bad actors around the world, America needs to be very careful about which conflicts it involves itself in. And the main threat to American interests on the world stage is clearly China. As any good statesman understands, foreign policy is more like a complex and strategic game of chess than a boxing match. One does not simply try to pummel opponents, but rather one looks for strategic (and often subtle) ways to gain an advantage and restrain one's enemies. A sensible foreign policy that recognizes the serious military, technological, and economic threat of China to the United States looks to avoid military conflict by seeking to implement policies that weaken and restrain China without provoking unnecessary conflict.

In 2024, Vance sponsored a bill to restrict China's ability to access US capital markets and exchanges if China fails to follow international laws related to trade, finance, and commerce.[37] This bill acknowledges something that is obvious to anyone paying attention to Chinese policy. China does not care very much about playing by the rules. From IP theft to allowing companies to essentially treat employees as slaves, China has many unfair advantages in the world economy.

The bill Vance proposed was quite simple. There were a number of specific international laws related to finance, trade, and commerce specified in the bill. It was stated that, if China was found to be in violation of such laws, the Secretary of the Treasury "shall prohibit any applicable United States entity, including capital markets, bond markets, and exchanges, from accepting any new investment, or effecting any transaction for others relating to a new investment, from such government or any commercial entities under the control of such government." The message was clear. China should no longer be free to violate international laws and essentially cheat the United States and still be treated by the United States as an equal economic partner. Actions have consequences.

Hopefully, this bill will be an example to Republicans as the situation with China continues to escalate. It is absurd and contrary to American interests to treat China as a harmless partner with whom we should continue to trade and do business when they violate international law and take advantage of American generosity. We should not provoke war, of course. But we need to make smart moves to keep China in check.

---

[37] A bill to restrict the Chinese Government from accessing United States capital markets and exchanges if it fails to comply with international laws relating to finance, trade, and commerce, S. 3945, 118th Cong. (2024), https://www.congress.gov/bill/118th-congress/senate-bill/3945/text.

The FAUCI Act

After several years of COVID policy, especially the rollout of the COVID vaccines and accompanying vaccine mandates, public health, and the relationship between big pharmaceutical companies and government agencies has come into the spotlight for good reason. When companies are positioned to make exorbitant amounts of money off of vaccines, and when governments and private entities attempt to pressure or require people to take those vaccines, it makes sense to look for links between those forcing the vaccines and those making a profit off of them.

In May 2024, Vance introduced the Fixing Administrations Unethical Corrupt Influence Act, not-so-subtly named the FAUCI Act, to address the particular concern about collusion between those who produce and sell vaccines and those who require people to receive them.[38] The bill would have prohibited former employees of the National Institutes of Health, the Food and Drug Administration, or the Centers for Disease Control and Prevention, "from serving on the board of entities involved in development and research of a drug, biological product, or device and from profiting from a drug, biological product, or device, and for other purposes."

The language of the bill was simple and banned three types of conduct for any former officials above a certain rank in government health agencies. First, these former officials were forbidden from serving on the board of companies that produce drugs or other medical products. Second, former federal employees of these agencies were forbidden from profiting from a drug or medical product when the person, while a federal employee, was

---

[38] FAUCI Act, S. 4232, 118th Cong. (2024), https://www.congress.gov/bill/118th-congress/senate-bill/4232/text.

involved in the approval of a grant to the company producing the drug or medical product. Third, certain former top officials of these agencies were forbidden from applying for certain medical patents.

It is important that law helps to prevent both actual corruption as well as *the appearance of corruption*, both of which harm the trust citizens have in their government. This bill would have accomplished both of those goals. The fluidity of people moving from government positions to the private sector while profiting off their government connections is real corruption. This bill would have prevented the obviously problematic situation of high-level officials in agencies like the FDA or NIH, who often have access to confidential information as well as power and influence, to become rich by peddling their influence in the private sector.

Besides actual corruption, there is a massive trust issue between citizens and government. Voters lose trust in their government when government officials are clearly using the information and connections that they gain from public service to enrich themselves. The fact that this may not be a simple case of personal enrichment, but may involve corrupt decisions to mandate certain vaccines or have government grants improperly favor certain drugs, there is a clear public harm. This bill would have been a simple way to keep public servants from harming the public and unjustly enriching themselves. Future Republican administrations should consider reintroducing this bill, as well as similar measures in other sectors, to prevent the peddling of government influence for private gain.

The Dismantle DEI Act

Another hot issue on which Vance proposed legislation is the "diversity, equity, and inclusion" regime in federal government. For decades, especially since the passage of the Civil Rights Act of 1964, various affirmative action programs have been in effect, often with government approval, in an attempt to remedy past discrimination. The result, ironically, has been the implementation of programs that clearly discriminate on the basis of race, sex, and other categories in the name of preventing discrimination.

The Dismantle DEI Act of 2024 was introduced to respond to this hypocritical use of discrimination in the name of preventing discrimination, to "ensure equal protection of the law, to prevent racism in the Federal Government, and for other purposes."[39] The main purpose of the act was to amend the Civil Rights Act of 1964 to ensure that no discriminatory act on the basis of race, ethnicity, religion, biological sex, and so on is permissible, even in the name of promoting "diversity, equity, and inclusion." The bill would have closed any DEI programs being administered by federal agencies and revoked several DEI-related executive orders signed by President Biden.

The details of the bill are less important than the general principle. Congress ought to assert its authority and act to end overt discrimination, which has been caused by affirmative action programs created by government agencies and sanctioned by courts for decades. Yes, DEI initiatives can be scrapped by executive order. Yes, recent Supreme Court rulings in the *Students for*

---

[39] Dismantle DEI Act of 2024, S. 4516, 118th Congr. (2024), https://www.congress.gov/bill/118th-congress/senate-bill/4516/text.

Fair Admission[40] cases have cut back judicial approval for affirmative action. But ultimately, Congress makes the laws and it is up to Congress to declare that DEI and affirmative action are impermissible instances of discrimination.

Ukraine Aid Transparency Act

One of Vance's priorities in the Senate, an issue on which he has consistently been a leader for years, is stopping (or at least questioning) the seemingly unrestricted flow of US aid to Ukraine in its war against Russia. While Vance acknowledged in early 2024 that cutting off aid to Ukraine altogether was not politically feasible, it was important to provide some accountability and take steps toward reining in (or at least making transparent) the extent to which the United States continued to fund a foreign military conflict.

In March 2024, Vance sponsored the Ukraine Aid Transparency Act.[41] The bill had one simple purpose. It required the government to provide a detailed accounting of all the money and weapons that had been supplied by the United States to Ukraine since the beginning of the war with Russia in February 2022. Depending on which source is relied on, as of early 2025 the United States had given (or pledged) somewhere between

---

[40] Students for Fair Admissions, Inc. v. President and Fellows of Harvard College, No. 20-1199, 600 U.S. ___ (2023).
[41] Ukraine Aid Transparency Act of 2024, S. 3903, 118th Cong. (2024), https://www.congress.gov/bill/118th-congress/senate-bill/3903/text.

$65 billion[42] and $175 billion[43] to Ukraine since 2022. The discrepancy and disagreement between the figures is part of the problem. The United States has been giving and pledging so many billions of dollars to Ukraine that it is hard to keep track of precisely how much has been given. Accountability is needed, both in principle—because government should be transparent and accountable about how it is spending taxpayer money—and in practice, to allow citizens to see precisely how much money the United States has spent on this foreign conflict. In order for voters to make informed decisions, they need accurate information about what their government is doing. This transparency bill would have allowed voters a clear and accurate picture of exactly how much aid our nation has been giving to Ukraine.

Illegal Immigration Bills

While Vance's proposed legislation focused on many policy areas, he sponsored several bills focused on fighting the illegal immigration crisis in the county. These various bills put forth by Vance are important because they show that he has consistently prioritized ending illegal immigration, but also because the proposed bills show creativity in dealing with the problems. Building a physical wall at the border and stopping the catch-and-release of people who show up at the border matter. But there are many other ways to disincentivize unlawful behavior.

---

[42] "U.S. Security Cooperation with Ukraine: Fact Sheet," *U.S. Department of State*, March 12, 2025, https://www.state.gov/bureau-of-political-military-affairs/releases/2025/01/u-s-security-cooperation-with-ukraine.

[43] Jonathan Masters and Will Merrow, "Here's How Much Aid the United States Has Sent Ukraine," *Council on Foreign Relations*, March 11, 2025, https://www.cfr.org/article/how-much-us-aid-going-ukraine.

In 2023, Vance sponsored the No Obamacare for Illegal Aliens Act.[44] The title of the bill speaks for itself. Since Obamacare is healthcare subsidized by the American taxpayer, the bill clarified that illegal immigrants would not be entitled to government-subsidized healthcare under the Affordable Care Act. This bill was introduced in response to a proposed rule issued by President Biden's Department of Health and Human Services, which expanded participation in government-subsidized healthcare plans like Obamacare and Medicaid to Deferred Action for Childhood Arrivals (DACA) participants who do not have legal status in the United States. While it should be common sense that government-subsidized benefits should be limited to legal citizens, in the current climate this bill made an important statement about disincentivizing illegal immigration.

In early 2024, Vance introduced the College Employment Accountability Act, which proposed to end any kind of federal funding for institutions of higher education that employed "unauthorized aliens."[45] The bill would have also required institutions of higher education to participate in E-Verify, a program that tracks the eligibility of non-citizens to lawfully work in the United States, in order to receive federal aid.

Also in early 2024, Vance sponsored a bill called the State Border Security Act.[46] The bill was introduced in response to the situation that was unfolding on the southern border. Border

---

[44] No Obamacare for Illegal Aliens Act, S. 2374, 118th Cong. (2023), https://www.congress.gov/bill/118th-congress/senate-bill/2374.
[45] College Employment Accountability Act, S. 3978, 118th Cong. (2024), https://www.congress.gov/bill/118th-congress/senate-bill/3978/text?s=1&r=7.
[46] State Border Security Act, S. 3668, 118th Cong. (2024), https://www.congress.gov/bill/118th-congress/senate-bill/3668/text.

states, alarmed by rampant illegal immigration and by the failure of the federal government to do anything about it, began to (modestly) take matters into their own hands by building fences on their borders with Mexico. The federal government unbelievably responded, not by doing its job and helping secure the border, but by filing lawsuits to make the border states remove the razor wire fencing they had put up. This bill proposed by Vance would have explicitly allowed border states to put up fencing at the border in order to deter illegal immigration and prevent the federal government from removing it.

These immigration bills show a common theme. Vance knows how to use modest, common-sense policies to make progress toward an important goal. Would any of these bills have stemmed the tide of illegal immigration? Not really. But these proposals add up. Yes, the ultimate resolution of mass illegal immigration comes when an administration is willing to put sufficient funds and manpower into comprehensively closing the border. But in the meantime, every angle of attack is helpful. When illegal immigrants (many of whom come from impoverished countries seeking financial improvement in America) cannot cross the border illegally and then receive government benefits, they are less likely to come here illegally in the first place. When colleges and universities are financially disincentivized from employing illegal immigrants, jobs are kept for American citizens and illegal immigrants cannot take them. When states are allowed to physically strengthen the southern border, there will be fewer gaps for illegal immigrants to cross. None of these policy proposals is a silver bullet, but each adds a layer of protection that disincentivizes illegal immigration. This is smart policy. Every small, calculated step toward an important goal is a step in the right direction.

Conclusion: A Legislative Roadmap for the Future

Vance's legislative priorities as a US senator show two things: his policy priorities and the sensible, incremental way he views the legislative progress. Both are important insights into who JD Vance is and how he thinks about politics and governing.

While this chapter sampled a few of the proposed bills Vance sponsored in the Senate and left out many others, the highlighted bills paint a picture of what Vance thinks is important for the good of the country. America needs a return to patriotism and unity among its citizens. Federal agencies need oversight just as much as private regulated businesses do. Corrupt use of positions in the federal government to make a profit in the private sector is dangerous and unacceptable. China is a threat that cannot be allowed to cheat America while we continue to grant our greatest geopolitical adversary favored status. Diversity, equity, and inclusion efforts are unlawful and intolerable if they involve discriminatory actions. America has been recklessly and unaccountably sending billions of dollars in aid to Ukraine, while the American people don't even know how much of their tax dollars are being sent there and for what purpose. America's bad policies encourage people to illegally cross the border and live in America.

Vance sees each of these issues—lack of patriotism, lack of accountability of federal agencies, government corruption, the threat of China, DEI, reckless involvement in foreign wars, and rampant illegal immigration—as serious threats to America's citizens, our institutions, and our way of life. It is encouraging to see that Vance, after spending years thinking, writing, and speaking intellectually about what ails America, actually went to the Senate and proposed legislation that sensibly addressed the problems he identified.

The policy priorities are almost less important than the tactical nature of each bill. Most of Vance's bills were not big cure-all statements attempting to provide a utopian solution to a major problem. Vance's legislative proposals were workable attempts to chip away at serious issues. Simply banning trade or commerce with China is not feasible. But setting parameters where China loses access to certain US markets if it breaks international laws is a concrete, realistic proposal to hold China accountable. Completely defunding aid to Ukraine in 2024 was not politically realistic. But passing a bill that forced the government to account for every dollar spent and every weapon sent to Ukraine would have shone a light on the extent of the irresponsible spending. One cannot simply pass a bill that ends the border crisis, but disincentivizing illegal immigrants by cutting off government benefits and access to jobs is an effective way to stop the flow of unlawful border crossings.

The Republicans were a minority in the Senate when Vance was a senator, so the bills discussed in this chapter were not enacted into law. But by reviewing the bills that Vance chose to write and sponsor, we get a glimpse into what he thinks are the most important political priorities for the good of the country. And we also learn that Vance is interested in intelligently and creatively finding workable solutions to policy problems. He is not interested in proposing big, flashy laws that pretend to solve problems. Vance's priorities and his practical ability to propose realistic solutions are a needed and refreshing skill set in today's Republican Party.

XII

Vance the Catholic Convert

What difference does an American politician's religion make? In the early years of the republic, the answer was quite a bit. Certain states and regions were extremely sectarian, sometimes even dominated by an established state church. Catholics frequently faced extreme prejudice. Often, they were looked upon with mistrust as insufficiently American because of their allegiance to the Pope. At the extremes, Catholics faced more than suspicion. Charles Carroll of Carrollton, the only Catholic signer of the Declaration of Independence, was unable to hold office or even to vote due to Maryland law.[47]

Things have changed quite a bit and religion does not have the same effect upon politics in the modern era. While the early republic was divided by denomination, with sects from

---

[47] Bradley J. Birzer, *American Cicero: The Life of Charles Carroll* (Intercollegiate Studies Institute, 2010).

Catholics to Mormons often distrusted and ostracized by mainline Protestants, today the interest of the voting public in the religion of political figures has very little to do with denomination. If people care at all, they wonder "what kind of religious person" a politician is. There are many liberal religious politicians—from liberal Catholics like Joe Biden and Nancy Pelosi to liberal Protestants like Senator Raphael Warnock. Some of them claim to take their social justice priorities from their religious faith, while others don't talk about religion much at all.

On the Right, there are a host of politicians from various sects and denominations who bring their religious faith into how they view everything from abortion and marriage to immigration policy. Today, the question of "what kind of religious person is this politician?" has less to do with his denomination than how his faith shapes his worldview. Politically conservative Catholics, evangelicals, and Mormons today often have similar faith-based worldviews, and therefore similar policy priorities, despite their vastly different theological beliefs.

However, the risk of the modern view is to limit consideration of religion in politicians to whether they are some kind of religious Conservative. Depth and intellect matter deeply. A politician might be deeply influenced by his religious faith, but have little grasp of the rich intellectual tradition of the faith. His policy preferences might be closely aligned with conservative religious voters, but the Christian intellectual tradition does little to actually form his thinking about politics and policy. Others, deeply influenced by the rich history of Christian social teaching, will think about politics and government quite differently.

Vance the Catholic Convert

Vance, as a Catholic convert, is not merely a Conservative politician who happens to be religious. Vance has clearly struggled with God, faith, theology, and the implications that these fundamental questions have for politics and the common good. As an adult Catholic convert, he has wrestled with the greatest questions about the existence of God and His will for man living together in community. Because he has taken these questions quite seriously and let the answers change his life by converting to Catholicism, we have in JD Vance a deep thinker who takes the principles of the Christian intellectual tradition quite seriously and who seeks to intelligently and reasonably apply those principles to the way he thinks about politics.

Before discussing Vance's religious worldview as a politician, however, it is worth diving into the actual story of his personal conversion. In 2020, Vance wrote a long, honest, and deep essay at the *Lamp* entitled "How I Joined the Resistance."[48] This is another candid piece that should be taken seriously; Vance had little to gain politically by divulging the inner thoughts and processes that led to him becoming a Catholic. Therefore, the essay is important for its raw honesty and depth of discussion on religious conversion.

The discussion of how Vance became a Catholic begins with a reflection about what his Mamaw, the person to whom he is most indebted for his successes in life, would think about his conversion to Catholicism. Mamaw was one of the most influential people in Vance's life, including on his early religious formation and views about faith. Mamaw was deeply religious in her

---

[48] "How I Joined the Resistance," *The Lamp*, April 1, 2020, https://thelampmagazine.com/blog/how-i-joined-the-resistance.

own way. She was also deeply skeptical of organized religion. She cared about Jesus but cared little for formal religious practices, like church attendance. Yet, perhaps surprisingly, Vance states that Mamaw was not particularly anti-Catholic either, as many Bible Belt Protestants tend to be.

Vance's reflection on Mamaw's view—and his own view as a boy—of Catholicism was mostly that it was a "little too stodgy, too formal." This is a deep insight into perhaps the root cause of anti-Catholic sentiment in much of middle America. While Vance grew up with some typical false Catholic stereotypes (Catholics worship Mary, they reject Scripture, and so on), this did not seem to be his central discomfort with Catholicism. He reflects on Catholic thought and Catholic art: Jesus is portrayed as God. He looms large, in many ways unlike normal folks, "wreathed in beams of light and crowned like a king." This made people like Vance uncomfortable: "The Catholic Jesus was a majestic deity, and we had little interest in majestic deities because we weren't a majestic people." Vance's people identified with ordinary folks and the Catholic Jesus didn't seem to be like ordinary folks. It seems the discomfort with Catholicism came less from hatred or deep theological disagreement and more from a sense that Catholicism was a high and majestic faith improper to ordinary hillbilly folks.

This sense of the otherness of Catholicism stayed with Vance as he started to consider the Catholic faith. Even as he began to overcome the intellectual barriers to Catholicism, Vance was left with this uneasiness. His reason led him toward Catholicism, yet he spent years on the edge, worried by the thought that "if I converted I would no longer be my grandmother's grandson." What would the woman who raised him, who loved Jesus but had no patience for high and mighty organized religion, think of JD becoming a Catholic?

After grappling with faith and religion as a young man, Vance went through a sadly typical progression. He was disaffected by the "prosperity gospel" style of Christianity he was encountering within Protestantism, a faith that promised earthly rewards in exchange for faithfulness. The dissatisfaction with this shallow religious view came from the reality that he saw so many good, prayerful people who suffered materially. If living the Gospel meant earthly success, why were so many Christians he knew suffering here on earth? Something wasn't adding up. That problem, coupled with the experience of serving in the Marine Corps, experiencing war, lacking a church community, going through the death of Mamaw, and finding himself in secular circles during his college and law school career, led Vance down a path toward atheism.

Yet despite the pull to atheism, a couple things held Vance back from the brink. First, he notes that to be an avowed atheist would be to separate himself from the cultural, religious, and conservative roots of his community and his people. He admits that most of them wouldn't care if he were an atheist, but there was something about believing in nothing that would be an "undeniable familial and cultural rupture" with his community. While Vance's people were not devout, they largely identified as Christians, and he did not want to completely sever that connection.

As his religious impulse continued to fade, Vance traded the religious connection to his community for a political one. By strongly affiliating with Republican Party politics, he could maintain common ground with his family and his culture. Yet as a non-believer, Vance was uncomfortable with many of the social conservative policy priorities within the conservative movement. So he attached himself to conservative economics and not to the conservative social issues that are so strongly bound to religion. It was easier to navigate his elite surroundings as an "economic Conservative." It may not have been acceptable to be religious among his elite colleagues, but he could maintain respectability while believing in limited government, tax cuts, and deregulation.

During this period of unbelief, Vance notes that his rejection of Christianity was less about intellectual disputes—such as the tensions between modern scientific theories and traditional religion—than about culture. As Vance moved into more elite crowds, it was simply easier to be an atheist. It is quite difficult for religious Conservatives to gain acceptance in the upper echelons of modern American society. As Aaron Renn pointed out in his commentary on the "three worlds of American evangelicalism," there has been a massive shift in the relationship between elite American culture and Christianity.[49] Until the 1960s, being a believing Christian was generally a positive for social position in America. But in the last decade or so, being a believing Christian is clearly a negative for one who wants to advance in high American society. So if one is not deeply convicted about one's faith and Christianity is a net negative for social and professional status, and when one constantly lives among peers who think Christianity is at best a harmless but foolish superstition, it is easy for religion to slowly fall away as an embarrassing inconvenience.

---

[49] Aaron M. Renn, "The Three Worlds of Evangelicalism Debate," *Aaron Renn*, May 18, 2022, https://www.aaronrenn.com/p/the-three-worlds-of-evangelicalism-7fc.

JD VANCE AND THE FUTURE OF THE REPUBLICAN PARTY

While Vance encountered some powerful philosophical arguments that challenged his atheism while in school, it seems it was more his relationships and his dissatisfaction with focusing primarily on professional success that turned his mind back toward God. He got into Yale Law School, climbed the ladder of elite society, and then fell in love. He realized that no amount of striving for achievement would accomplish what he wanted most: "a happy, thriving family." He realized that what he wanted was not simply to achieve material success, but to be good. As Vance grappled with what that meant, he realized it had more to do with virtue and self-sacrifice than with professional achievement.

While Vance continued strive for material success, he realized that he also had a growing desire to have a better character. He wanted to be able to control his temper, put the interests of his loved ones above his own, and become a man who would be a good, patient, loving husband and father. During this conversion process, Vance came across a beautiful passage from St. Augustine commenting on the book of Genesis. There is much to comment on in the passage and Vance's reaction to it, but one important thought from St. Augustine stands out: "In matters that are obscure and far beyond our vision...different Interpretations are sometimes possible without prejudice to the faith we have received. In such a case, we should not rush in headlong and so firmly take our stand on one side that, if further progress in the search of truth justly undermines this position, we too fall with it." This truth hit Vance hard. Most of the hang-ups and supposed contradictions between faith and modern science and thought are often the result, not of inherent contradictions, but of imperfect understanding in the person trying to reconcile the two. Truth is always true; if the Faith is true, then it is reconcilable with all that is true in science, in politics, and in all of the natural world. Any apparent contradiction comes not from the Faith being false but from an imperfect understanding of either the Faith or of science. This reflection transformed Vance's understanding of the depth, the reasonableness, and the truth of Christian faith. The imperfection was in his imperfect humanity trying to understand both faith and the world around him, not in the Christian faith itself.

The other pivotal moment for Vance during law school came not from a book, but from an encounter with a person. Peter Thiel, the now-famous venture capitalist, came to Yale Law and gave a talk on campus. Thiel spoke about the cutthroat competition among elite students for the same prestigious clerkships and law firm jobs, coupled with the stagnation of technological advancement in modern society. Because there was no technological advancement in areas that mattered (travel and infrastructure, cures for terminal diseases, efficient energy use, and so on), Thiel argued that elites were left without hope of using their talents and their education to have a truly transformative effect on society and humanity. So, they turn their ambitions to competing with one another "over a dwindling number of prestigious outcomes." This talk led Vance to reflect further on his obsession with achievement and to wonder what he should really be striving for.

The meaninglessness of striving for professional prestige above all else started to dawn on Vance. He had been viewing the fight for the right clerkship and the right job "not as an end to something meaningful, but to win a social competition." He realized that he didn't even really know why he cared about such things. Why did he want a job at a prestigious law firm where he would work long hours doing work he probably wouldn't like? "I looked to the future, and realized that I'd been running a desperate race where the first prize was a job I hated." When the goal didn't look so good, his confidence that he was on the right path started to waver.

These reflections from Thiel changed Vance's professional path, leading him to start planning for a career outside of the practice of law. But the interaction with Thiel had another effect. Peter Thiel was both a Christian and "possibly the smartest person I'd ever met." The stereotype that simple people were Christians and that really smart people were nonbelievers was shattered by this encounter with one brilliant man who identified as a Christian.

Vance was introduced by Peter Thiel to the philosophy of René Girard, and particularly to Girard's understanding of the scapegoat. In Jesus Christ, the truth of the scapegoat is revealed: the one who is innocent, the one who has not wronged society, accepts the blame and the punishment for all human sin and violence. The moral failings of humanity are revealed, accepted, and healed by Christ. Christ, the innocent scapegoat, forces us to look at our own failings honestly rather than shifting blame onto someone else. Christ is not a mythical symbolic way for people to deal with the hardships of life. He is real, the true answer to the question of the meaning of life. He is the one way to make sense of a fallen world that could be redeemed. This insight transformed Vance's inner life: "It was time to stop scapegoating and focus on what I could do to improve things." This thought came to Vance just as he was pondering his own story and writing *Hillbilly Elegy*. As Vance reflected on Christ as well as his own failings, the story of *Hillbilly Elegy* was transformed from an angry, resentful story of triumph over the failings of his family (especially his mother) to a humbler and more complex tale of a life, a community, and an outlook on society that provided no easy answers. Bringing Christ into the story allowed Vance to see beyond the apparent meaninglessness of his people's suffering and to hope for redemption. Vance's conversion transformed the telling of his own story, as well as the rest of his life.

This transformation led Vance to see the failings of both the Right and Left when discussing modern social problems. The Right spoke correctly about cultural and personal deficiencies, but was sometimes a bit heartless in failing to acknowledge the tragic forces at play. The worldview of many on the Right gave too much power to personal responsibility and overlooked the realities of sin, the fallen world, and the effect that sin has on institutions. The Left kept talking about the systemic problems and the need for more resources, while failing to acknowledge that material well-being did not seem to fix the most destructive forces plaguing families and communities. If the Right lacked compassion, the compassion of the Left failed to see hope that individuals could transcend their circumstances. The Left's philosophy "reeked of giving up."

This realization of the insufficiency of both the modern Right or Left to understand the deepest problems of human life was for Vance a moment of grace. He sought "a worldview that understood our bad behavior as simultaneously social and individual, structural and moral." He needed a lens through which to look upon the world that was clearer and more complete than the political philosophies he was encountering in his elite world. Struggling to find that worldview, he remembered Mamaw, the woman who had already shown him both that life isn't fair and that he could still do something about it. And Mamaw was a Christian; her Christianity is what gave her that wisdom. That wisdom recognized sin, which gave an accurate name to all "the behaviors I had seen destroy lives and communities." Mamaw's Christianity explained her simple view of politics that had been so foreign and seemingly incongruent to Vance growing up. She supported Democrats who spoke on behalf of the poor, the downtrodden, and the worker. Yet she had many socially conservative instincts and she did not like cries of helplessness that discounted the power of individuals to work hard and rise up.

Mamaw's Christianity helped complete Vance's political thought, his struggle for personal virtue, and his desires for systemic change. Sin and grace do what individual choice and systemic reform alone cannot do: account for the mystery of both personal and communal weakness and failure.

As Vance became increasingly dissatisfied with the state of modern society and continued his journey of conversion, he found the best diagnosis of our modern ills, not in a contemporary author, but in St. Augustine's 1500-year-old *City of God*. Augustine describes the decadent state of Roman society. When society is focused on consumption and pleasure as the chief goods to be obtained, duty and virtue fall by the wayside. This insight spoke to Vance of both the fundamental modern problem and the solution. The fundamental modern problem was a focus on consumption and material well-being as the primary metric of success. The solution was a Christian life of virtue, holiness, and happiness in the highest sense. This revelation, coupled with Vance encountering conservative thinkers like Oren Cass who were willing to question conservative orthodoxy by denying that consumption should be the primary measure of political good, transformed Vance into the Conservative he has become over the past several years.

This shifting worldview also "ultimately led not just to Christianity, but to Catholicism." Despite the fact that Mamaw was no Catholic, Vance began to conclude that Catholic thought was

> the closest expression of her kind of Christianity: obsessed with virtue, but cognizant of the fact that virtue is formed in the context of a broader community; sympathetic with the meek and poor of the world without treating them primarily as victims; protective of children and families and with the things necessary to ensure they thrive. And above all: a faith centered around a Christ who demands perfection of us even as He loves unconditionally and forgives easily.

Like many religious converts, Vance had no "aha moment" but rather a series of conversations, relationships, interactions, and insights that slowly led him down the path to the Catholic Church. He realized that Mamaw's life was more compatible with Catholic theology than any other religious system. He encountered Peter Thiel, the writings of St. Augustine and René Girard, the example of a Catholic uncle who married into the family and was the most virtuous Christian Vance had ever met. Vance was convinced that the Catholic Church's teachings were reasonable, that they were true, that they answered his deepest questions about personal and communal life, and that they offered the path to a virtuous, happy, and good life.

So after years of discerning and struggling, Vance became a Catholic. This certainly shapes the vision with which he views the world, as it should. But it is not just about intellectual vision. The faith changed Vance into an intellectual who realized that the intellectual life is necessary but not sufficient for the believer. The Church is also "about the heart, as well, and the community of believers. It's about going to Mass and receiving the Sacraments, even when it's difficult or awkward to do so. It's about so many things that I'm ignorant of, and the process of becoming less ignorant over time." Perhaps one of the great effects on Vance was the introduction of this humility. Vance is a brilliant man who climbed his way from a poor, dysfunctional family life into one of the most prestigious law schools in the world and eventually into the vice presidency of the United States. He was used to knowing a lot, succeeding a lot, and being among the best. His conversion to Catholicism, his introduction to a deep tradition of 2,000 years of philosophy, theology, spiritual insight, and wisdom, led him to realize how much more there is to learn and to become. That humility is necessary for a good leader and true statesman to become great.

Vance's embrace of his moral duty to be patient with his kids, control his temper, be a good husband and father, and prefer the good of his family to career ambition, is an essential quality in a leader. Religious faith in political leaders is not simply beneficial because of the policy preferences to which religious faith often leads. Seeking virtue, desiring patience, listening well, remaining humble, always learning, and seeking the public good rather than private gain are qualities that separate great leaders from self-serving politicians. When Vance reflects on his need to not only be an intellectual Catholic, but to pray more, receive God's grace, and become the person that God desires him to be, it should be cause for great hope. A great leader needs virtue, not merely the right policy positions or political instincts. Therefore, Vance's religious conversion is not merely an interesting personal fact but a promising sign of a leader who will continue to grow in all the right ways.

Vance the Catholic VP

Five years after Vance converted to Catholicism and wrote about his religious conversion at the *Lamp*, he was sworn in as vice president of the United States. Does his faith shape the way he looks at politics and government? And if so, how?

In January 2025, Vance gave an interview on Fox News—and then went viral in some debates on Twitter/X—about the traditional Christian concept of the *ordo amoris* (the order of love) and its application to the America first immigration agenda in America.

This exchange reveals something fascinating (and to Christians, something exciting) about Vance. He takes the Catholic intellectual tradition seriously. He wants to apply the wisdom of Christian tradition to contemporary issues. Despite complaints that Vance misinterpreted Catholic doctrine, his discussion of the *ordo amoris* stands firmly and intelligently within Catholic tradition. The concept of the *ordo amoris* was first explored by St. Augustine, a major intellectual influence on Vance's conversion. And St. Thomas Aquinas explores this topic at length in the Summa Theologica.[50] Catholic teaching has much to say about charity. Do we owe an identical amount of charity to all people—parents, spouses, family, neighbors, and strangers? No, such a concept is inhuman and impossible. Theologians may quibble, but Vance does not need to be a theologian to rely on his faith to analyze an issue. The simple observation that we cannot owe the

---

[50] Saint Thomas Aquinas, *Summa Theologica Part II-II*, Q26, A8.

same amount and type of love to every person in the world as we owe to our families is sound.

It is quite encouraging to see a public political figure, the vice president of the United States, grappling seriously with questions of policy through the lens of philosophy and moral theology. Vance is not simply using Scripture verses or relying on revelation to make a rhetorical point. He is also not using an argument from authority and declaring "God says this is the way it is, so that is the way we will govern." His thinking is not arbitrary nor unreasonable. But in exploring and enacting government policies, Vance is making a concerted effort to seek the truth at the highest level. He is not just relying on political expediency. Rather, his political analysis includes grappling seriously with questions of what is true and good, and then trying to apply the answers to politics. It is refreshing to see a political figure engaging publicly with deep questions of religious faith and trying to put that faith into practice in the act of governing.

This classical tradition of Christian statesmanship is in need of recovery, especially in America. There are two common and unfortunate trends in modern politics regarding religion. Both are distinct from Vance's public religious persona and thought.

One is secularism (an ideology sadly held by both nonbelievers and a number of believers as well), which holds that religious beliefs and arguments have little to no place in politics, government, and the public square. Secularism has convinced many people, including more than a few on the Right, that religious beliefs are meant to be private and that such beliefs do not belong in discussions about public policy. This is a modern novelty, not a conservative principle. But it is a powerful force within modern political discourse.

The other is a kind of populist religiosity, particularly among Protestants in certain regions, where politicians hold religious values, speak about them openly, and apply them to the way they vote and govern. This is not bad—in fact, it is a perfectly reasonable way for politicians who are also deeply religious to behave. But it tends to be more about connecting with voters through rhetoric and issues that reflect Christian beliefs than articulating those beliefs on a deep, policy-related level.

Vance is doing something distinct from this. Vance is helping to bring back the classical Christian tradition of statesmanship and government. Political leaders do not need to be academics or professional philosophers, but they ought to seriously engage with the intellectual tradition, history, philosophy, theology, and so on, so that the greatest wisdom developed and collected over many centuries helps form their way of governing.

One final distinction is between cultural Christianity and Christianity truly believed; embracing Christianity because it is useful and embracing it because it is true are two very different things. In February 2025, Vance gave an interview at the CPAC conference,[51] where he talked about what Christian faith means and made it very clear where he stands. He began his remarks on the issue by pointing out that "I believe the fundamental tenet of the Christian faith. It's not just a set of good moral principles...the fundamental tenet of our faith is that the Son of God became man. He died and then He raised Himself from the dead." To Christians, this point may seem obvious. But in today's political discourse, it is important that Vance made this statement. From major political figures like former UK Prime

---

[51] CPAC Interview, February 20, 2025, https://x.com/megbasham/status/1892659115144409378.

Minister Liz Truss and French President Emmanuel Macron to modern cultural icons like Richard Dawkins, many prominent people have praised the cultural value of Christianity. They may be too enlightened to believe in the existence of God and the core teachings of Christianity, but they think the teachings of Christianity are valuable for strong communities, a stable social order, and so on.

Vance distinguishes himself from cultural Christianity by making clear that he is actually a believing Christian. He does not simply think Christianity is admirable or useful; he believes it is true. And "so much flows from that" central belief. God really became man in the person of Jesus Christ. For the believer, there is no reason to fear death. Losing one's soul is much worse than losing one's physical life. The fact that Vance actually believes this means we can trust that he fears sinning against the truth more than he fears losing a political battle (or even losing his life). The fear of God and the commitment to truth and goodness that transcends earthly desires is a powerful quality in the mind and heart of a politician.

So what does this serious, devout faith mean for governance? Does it mean Vance advocates for government intervention to push religious faith and make America a Christian nation? While Christian Nationalists and Catholic integralists might hope so, Vance's aspiration is simpler and more moderate. The purpose of good government is to create "the space where moms and dads can raise their children in their faith to become good young people." Government cannot force faith. But it can create a society where parents can raise children to become good, faithful citizens without political or cultural disincentives. Government can ensure that barriers to religious faith—whether in the form of bad government policy or anti-religious institutions—do not interfere with the ability of parents to raise their children well.

Vance ends this portion of his interview by reminding people what it means to be a faithful Christian: "we put our faith in God above. We put our faith in the grace of God and we try our best to do His will. And we don't worry so much about whether we're going to have earthly rewards. We worry about whether we're doing right by God Almighty above. That's what I try to do and that's how I try to run my life in public." This insight may not explain exactly what Vance would do about each area of policy. But it is a needed quality in a political leader. Vance believes he has a duty to do what is right and that his primary concern is not whether he has earthly success, but whether he is doing God's will. In an age where so many political leaders are focused on popularity, staying in power, and cultivating their own political careers, we need less self-service and more political courage. We need politicians who care more about doing what is good in the eyes of God than in achieving earthly success. Instilling this mentality in our present and future political leaders could completely change the state of American politics.

One final note: Vance is new to the Catholic faith. So it is both inaccurate and unfair to categorize him as a statesman of mature, well-integrated religious faith. In his speech at the National Catholic Prayer Breakfast in 2025, he movingly and humbly admitted this:

> I recognize very much that I am a "baby Catholic"—that there are things about the faith that I don't know. So I try to be humble as best I can when I talk about the faith…publicly, because of course, I'm not always going to get

it right. And I don't want my inadequacies in describing our faith to fall back on the faith itself. And so if you ever hear me pontificating about the Catholic faith, please recognize it comes from a place of deep belief, but it also comes from a place of not always knowing everything all the time.[52]

So Vance is young in his faith and liable to make mistakes. His practice and application of the faith in politics will not be perfect. But the fact that he has the genuine faith of a convert and is willing to grapple seriously with it, including in his public political life, is a good sign for faith in America. It is good to have a leader who takes Christian faith so seriously, because of the effect that faith will have on his leadership and for the example it will set for our future leaders.

---

[52] "Full Text: Vice President JD Vance at the 2025 National Catholic Prayer Breakfast," *National Catholic Register*, February 28, 2025, https://www.ncregister.com/news/jd-vance-full-speech-national-catholic-prayer-breakfast-2025-5bcglky9.

XIII

Towards a New Republican Party

While times and circumstances can change and bring about the unexpected, there is enough information gleaned from essays, speeches, and other reflections in the preceding chapters to paint a picture of what a future JD Vance presidency. We can get a glimpse into what the future of the Republican Party looks like after Trump. Any conversation about the future needs to focus on an area where major changes are underway: foreign policy priorities.

Vance and the Foreign Policy of the New Republican Party

The Republican Party is moving away from the neoconservative leanings of the past few decades. There is less interest in America functioning as the world police, and more interest in limiting US involvement in foreign affairs to situations that directly affect the American interest. Vance has been a leader in this move toward a less interventionist, more realistic and restrained US foreign policy.

In the 2024 essay *The Republican Plot Against Donald Trump*,⁵³ Vance laid out the essence of his views on foreign policy. While foreign policy is often discussed in clichés and extreme caricatures, Vance's take is realistic, reasonable, and representative of the views of a growing number of American voters. While Vance is indeed a refreshing change from the neoconservative wing of the Republican Party and its hawkish posture toward foreign conflict, Vance is no isolationist. So what, practically, do "restraint" and "foreign policy realism" look like? The conversation requires a serious reflection on what it means for foreign policy action, including military involvement, to be in the American interest.

As a senator, Vance was consistently one of the most skeptical members of Congress regarding continued American aid to Ukraine in its war with Russia. Despite the unfair attacks from opponents, who claimed that opposition to Ukraine aid meant support of Vladimir Putin and Russian aggression, Ukraine skepticism from Americans means no such thing. There is a false dichotomy that has been presented since the war began in 2022 that America must either pour its own resources into support of Ukraine's war effort or America outwardly supports Vladimir Putin's invasion of Ukraine. But it is quite possible for Americans to disapprove of Putin's actions—just as most right-thinking

---

⁵³ JD Vance, "The Republican Plot Against Donald Trump," *The American Conservative*, February 12, 2024, https://www.theamericanconservative.com/how-congress-is-pursuing-endless-war-in-ukraine-and-trying-to-stop-a-trump-election/.

people will disapprove of dozens of conflicts all across the globe—without believing that it is in America's interest to send billions of dollars to Ukraine to support its war effort. It is completely legitimate for America to stay out of foreign wars, even if one side seems to have a just cause.

Vance has been an important voice for this position of American restraint. It is very important for powerful voices in American politics to stand up and question why the nation is spending so much money on foreign wars that do not seem to directly affect the interests of ordinary Americans. As budget deficits and the national debt continue to soar to unbelievable levels, it is a patriotic duty to ask why we are spending money we don't have to aid Ukraine in a war with Russia, thousands of miles from America's borders—especially when our own border is unsecured and remains an existential threat to the future of the nation.

Vance's foreign policy stances are neither those of a neoconservative war hawk nor an isolationist—another false dichotomy that needs to be eliminated from public discourse. Vance's skepticism about continuing to fund the war in Ukraine does not come from an isolationist desire for America to remain neutral and stay out of all foreign affairs. Vance laid out his vision for an "America first" foreign policy in an April 2024 interview on Fox News Sunday.[54] Vance made two things clear. America is stretched too thin in its foreign policy commitments and funding the war is not in the American interest.

First, America simply cannot print weapons, ammunition, and the supplies necessary to wage war the way it can print

---

[54] Fox News Interview, April 28, 2024, https://www.foxnews.com/video/6351929463112.

money. There are serious conflicts brewing—particularly with China—that will directly impact America's interest. We simply cannot be involved in every conflict around the world and still maintain the military readiness necessary for an actual war that we could be forced to fight. For that reason alone, sending money and arms to a conflict like the Russia-Ukraine war is imprudent in the absence of a direct American interest.

Second, it is Europe, not America, that has a direct interest in this conflict. If one grants that Russia is an unjust aggressor and Ukraine's cause is righteous, this remains a regional conflict in eastern Europe. Those who fear that Putin's ambitions are imperial and go beyond Ukraine are concerned that he may next target Lithuania and Poland, not New York and Washington, DC. Reasonable minds may disagree about the strategic importance of countering an aggressive Russia, but it is offensive to assume that the *only* patriotic response to a war in eastern Europe is American involvement. Acting as if supporting Ukraine is the only reasonable American reaction is naive and shuts down a serious and necessary conversation about the role of America in foreign affairs that do not directly involve the interests of the United States.

So if we need to analyze America's foreign involvement and prioritize only what is directly in our nations' interest, what does that mean? On the world stage, the focus clearly should be China. Vance was clear in the Fox News interview that China has both the ambition and the power to challenge America on the world stage. We do not have limitless resources (either in dollars or in weapons) and we should be very concerned that America has been giving away precious resources to Ukraine since 2022 while China continues to be a threat. Russia doesn't seem to have the power to seriously challenge or affect America, while China threatens the US on many levels. China is making a real effort to replace the dollar as the world reserve currency. It continues to steal western intellectual property. And China makes serious claims about sovereignty over Taiwan, which has geopolitical importance due to its location as well as its production of semiconductors. America cannot fight every aggressor around the world that starts a conflict. It is clearly in the American interest to be concerned about the rise of China. It is hardly clear that Russia presents such a threat to the American interest.

Further, a prudent foreign policy acknowledges that the American interest requires focusing on problems close to home. The nation has its own borders to worry about, which has been a major focus of Vance's political action over the last couple years. Vance is obviously not the only one emphasizing the need to secure the US-Mexico border. But it is clear that Vance sees this, not merely as a popular domestic issue to fire up the MAGA base, but as a *foreign policy* issue. Vance's skepticism about funding the war in Ukraine is intimately related to his hawkishness about securing the southern border, getting illegal immigration under control, and fixing the rampant abuses of the asylum system. America should be involved with foreign nations, whether through economic means or military force, only when the issue directly affects America's interest. Of course, there will always be debate about how direct the American interest needs to be to justify involvement, but in this case the dichotomy is quite clear. The American interest in the Russia-Ukraine war is nebulous and debatable. The American interest in stopping millions of people from illegally crossing from Mexico to the United States, sometimes bringing with them human trafficking rings, violent gang activity, and drugs, is obvious. The war in Ukraine may be in the American interest in some sense. But the southern border is clearly *the* foreign policy crisis in modern American life.

The Monroe Doctrine, first articulated by President Monroe in 1823, generally states that European nations should not meddle in the Americas and that America should stay out of the wars of European powers. While the doctrine has been used to justify US intervention abroad (in ways that might surprise President Monroe and his Secretary of State John Quincy Adams), the Monroe Doctrine remains relevant when used properly. It was a coherent and persuasive idea to keep nineteenth century America out of European imperial conflicts and, more recently, to justify American intervention when the Soviet Union set its sights on Cuba. The Monroe Doctrine states that nations should be much more concerned with and involved in foreign affairs that occur in their own backyards than those that take place halfway around the world.

To be fair, times have changed since President Monroe; we live in a hi-tech, globalized society. In an age of intercontinental ballistic missiles and high-speed aircraft, foreign wars halfway around the world can indeed have a direct effect on the United States—which is why China's interest in Taiwan is a legitimate foreign policy concern. But as a general rule, Vance is correct that we would do better to look at the regions and nations around us before looking too far abroad. When drugs and crime are pouring across an unsecured US-Mexico border that stretches nearly 2,000 miles, that is of primary concern. Another primary concern is the hostile maneuvering of China, because America has become so reliant on the manufacturing and trading power (not to mention the debt financing) of China. But when America has limited resources, both financial and military, to expend on foreign conflicts, it is legitimate to question why we would prioritize involvement in a dispute over the Russia-Ukraine border. The Russia-Ukraine dispute is simply too far from home and too indirectly related to the American interest to be a primary concern.

Vance is well within the laudable American tradition of foreign policy realism and restraint—from the non-intervention of George Washington[55] to the doctrine of James Monroe—when he suggests that we should untangle ourselves from Ukraine and prioritize our own southern border and our main geopolitical rival in China. "We cannot fight every war and take a side in every conflict; we must prioritize" is not isolationism nor is it support of tyranny. It is merely a legitimate recognition that America does not have unlimited resources, does not have a direct interest in every military conflict in the world, and needs to focus on its own priorities.

Domestic Policy

In February 2025, JD Vance made headlines for the brilliant speech he gave at the Munich Security Conference.[56] One of the lines that garnered much media attention serves as a good segue from foreign to domestic policy:

> We gather at this conference, of course, to discuss security. And normally we mean threats to our external security.... But while the Trump administration is very concerned with European

---

[55] "Washington's Farewell Address," *Office of the Historian*, September 17, 1796, https://history.state.gov/milestones/1784-1800/washington-farewell.

[56] "Read: J.D. Vance's full speech on the decline of Europe," *The Spectator World*, February 14, 2025, https://thespectator.com/topic/read-jd-vance-full-speech-decay-europe/.

> security and believes that we can come to a reasonable settlement between Russia and Ukraine, and we also believe that it's important in the coming years for Europe to step up in a big way to provide for its own defense, the threat that I worry the most about vis-à-vis Europe is not Russia, it's not China, it's not any other external actor. What I worry about is the threat from within. The retreat of Europe from some of its most fundamental values....

Yes, war is frightening and a threat to the security of free nations. Yes, there are external threats to America's safety and its future, especially the threat of a rising China. But Vance knows that the biggest threat to our nation and Western civilization generally, is "the threat from within." This threat to American values and American flourishing comes in many forms: the corruption of American institutions, the lack of unifying patriotism among Americans, the offshoring and elimination of good jobs for the American middle class, DEI policies, the collapse of religion and stable family formation, drug and pornography epidemics, and excessive spending and debt. JD Vance has a clear vision of what is wrong with American life today—he is well aware of the threat from within. But what would President Vance do to fix it? What policy platform is the Republican Party going to adopt in the years and decades to come to address America's domestic crises?

As Vance has made clear for years, his focus is on fostering a pro-family and pro-worker nation where it is easier to form a stable family, raise healthy children, and engage in meaningful work to support a family. While policy covers diverse topics—tax policy, government regulation, trade, educational funding, welfare benefits, and much more—we can expect that Vance will view all areas of policy through the lens of what will benefit the American family and the American worker.

Vance credits Trump's instincts as crucial to starting this realignment in Republican politics, but says that this alone is "not enough to build a political movement around."[57] In his speech, Vance noted that policy changes are needed to address new circumstances, new problems, and new institutional decay. The movement to form a conservative platform and the detailed policy proposals necessary to address twenty-first century America are still being worked out. So while Vance has been a leader in articulating the biggest problems facing the nation today and the ways in which the Republican Party needs to adapt to address them, some of the details will likely be worked out in debate and creative legislation in the years to come. Still, we can piece together some areas of policy where we are likely to see Vance focus his efforts.

Pro-Family Policy

Vance clearly wants to see the Republican Party focus on pro-family policy. Particularly, he wants to see policies that make it easier for people to get married and have children. The Republican Party has been split on this in recent years. While some, like Vance, want to see government policy that actively seeks to promote marriage and children, libertarian-leaning Conservatives are skeptical of government spending and intervention, even for the good end of promoting family formation.

---

[57] Sen. J.D. Vance, "Towards a Pro-Worker, Pro-Family Conservatism," *The American Conservative*, May 29, 2019, https://www.theamericanconservative.com/towards-a-pro-worker-pro-family-conservatism/.

With Vance as a leader, we can expect to see Republicans move toward putting creative, pro-family, natalist policies into action. What, precisely, might that look like?

Vance has openly advocated for some particular policies to promote families having more children in the past.[58] He has called for a higher child tax credit, raising the credit from $2,000 to $5,000 per child. He has also expressed interest in a government program instituted in Hungary, where newly married couples are eligible for a loan that is forgivable if the couple has three or more children.[59] Vance asks: if a lack of children in America is a "civilizational crisis" and there are couples who would like to have more kids but can't afford it, why does our government not try creative solutions to give those families more resources?

There are two common objections to such pro-family fiscal proposals from Republicans: government involvement in these areas is improper or the proposals won't work.

Spending proposals that try to increase birth rates is a challenge for Republicans who have categorically distrusted and dismissed government solutions to societal problems. But the reality is we have a government; we have taxes; we have government spending programs. Any such program should be aimed at achieving the common good. And there is perhaps no societal good more important than promoting stable families and increasing birth rates in this country. The very fate of the nation

---

[58] Joseph Zeballos-Roig, "Vance wants to be a 'pro-family' Republican. His party isn't there yet." *Semafor*, October 3, 2024, https://www.semafor.com/article/10/02/2024/vance-wants-a-pro-family-republicanism-his-party-isnt-there-yet.

[59] "JD Vance on our Civilizational Crisis," Speech by JD Vance, July 4, 2021, Posted September 7, 2021, by Intercollegiate Studies Institute. YouTube, 22:53. https://www.youtube.com/watch?v=jBrEng3xQYo&t=1372s.

depends on having enough children to maintain the population. Vance is willing to be a leader, to be creative, and to experiment with policies that will promote this goal of stronger families with more children. "If we are not willing to spend resources to solve it, we are not serious about the very real problem that we face. So we should do it. We should give resources to parents who are going to have kids. We should make it easier to raise American families. And we should send the signal to the culture that we are the pro-family party and we are going to back it up with real policy."

The second criticism, that "these policies won't work," may be valid in the end. But there is a simple response: "well, maybe that is true. But the problem is dire and we need to try." Vance does not speak with certainty about any particular family policy; he proposes no silver-bullet solution. Increasing tax credits may encourage some families to have additional children. Forgivable loans might help families who want more children to make the decision. Yes, in the end the low birth rates are caused primarily by culture and not money. But even if the results of implementing these policies are modest, the lack of births in America (and most Western nations) is a civilizational crisis and it is worth spending resources and experimenting to try to move the needle. It is worth trying something rather than doing nothing. And in any event, there is a prudent opportunity here to reform existing welfare programs into these pro-family programs, so that our current welfare policies are transformed from programs that enable poverty to programs that incentivize keeping families together and having children.

We should expect Vance to take family stability and birth rates seriously and to experiment with government programs, like tax credits and forgivable loans, in order to encourage more

Americans to get married, stay married, and have more children. If he believes the birth rate problem is truly a civilizational crisis, we can expect some risk and experimentation with policies that try to solve it.

Workers and Manufacturing

Vance wants to enable as many Americans as possible to achieve the American Dream of marrying and having a stable family. The other part of the American Dream equation is to provide for as many Americans as possible the opportunity to obtain meaningful work that can provide for that family. While this means enacting policies that stimulate the economy and encourage investment and entrepreneurship, this is only a partial, white-collar answer.

We want a nation where white-collar professionals can thrive, create jobs, drive productivity, and increase wealth. And yes, those white-collar opportunities can trickle down to better job opportunities for the lower and middle classes. From his time in the venture capital world, Vance has seen the power of technology and innovation to create wealth. And he has seen that, when entrepreneurs are free to create, their creations drive job and wage growth opportunities for others. That is part of why Vance left Silicon Valley, so he could return to Ohio and try to encourage investors to invest in these middle American towns, so that those towns could provide meaningful opportunities and better work. We should expect that Vance will continue the Republican theme of trying to cut taxes and regulations in a way that allows private sector entrepreneurship to drive economic growth.

But ultimately, Vance understands that a powerhouse American economy, that provides meaningful jobs at a living wage for as many workers as possible, means bringing as much manufacturing back to the United States as possible. Given that this is a priority, I would expect to see the Republican platform and administrations in coming years experiment with different methods that entice manufacturers to bring operations (back) to the United States. This will likely consist of both positive and negative incentives for reshoring. Tax holidays of some sort—tax credits or abatements for companies who bring overseas manufacturing operations back to America—are likely. Of course, this is not a cure all. But there will be businesses whose decision to offshore manufacturing only resulted in a marginal financial benefit. So a tax holiday for those companies may do just enough to incentivize them to bring manufacturing jobs back to the United States.

If tax holidays are the positive incentive for reshoring manufacturing jobs, protective tariffs are the negative side of the coin. It is hard to sort through the many conflicting studies—tariffs either help bring jobs back to America and bring in revenue in the process,[60] or it is a toss-up and they may or may not work,[61] or they are a "dumb idea" that will not reshore American jobs.[62] I am not an economist, but it is worth seriously exploring the

---

[60] "Fact Sheet: President Donald J. Trump Restores Section 232 Tariffs," The White House, February 11, 2025, https://www.whitehouse.gov/fact-sheets/2025/02/fact-sheet-president-donald-j-trump-restores-section-232-tariffs/.

[61] Sara Savat, "Tariffs may not bring global supply chains back; WashU research explains," *WashU The Source*, February 10, 2025, https://source.washu.edu/2025/02/tariffs-may-not-bring-global-supply-chains-back-washu-research-explains/.

[62] Terence Corcoran, "'Reshoring,' the dumb idea behind tariffs," *Financial Post*, March 7, 2025, https://financialpost.com/opinion/terence-corcoran-reshoring-the-dumb-idea-behind-tariffs.

value of protective tariffs as a tool to restore the American manufacturing base.

First, the idea simply makes sense. If companies that rely heavily on sales to American markets will pay a steep tax to export their products from foreign nations to America, it will often make financial sense for those companies to move their manufacturing operations to America and forego paying the tariff. Some critics point to the likely increase in the cost of goods that will result, while other critics focus on the negative effect tariffs may have on GDP.[63] Again, I'm not an economist, but the first criticism needs to take the tradeoff seriously. If the price of some goods rise but in exchange there is a new burst of high-paying middle-class jobs for American workers, the benefit may very well outweigh the cost.

The criticism about the negative effect that tariffs or other economic policies may have on GDP is an important conversation finally taking place within the conservative movement. Vance (and thinkers like Oren Cass) have been attempting to shift the conversation for years by looking at economic success in different terms.[64] In response to the belief that GDP defines a nation's economic success, perhaps the Right should refocus on something deeper and more real to average Americans.

---

[63] "The Fiscal, Economic, and Distributional Effects of 20% Tariffs on China and 25% Tariffs on Canada and Mexico," *The Budget Lab*, March 3, 2025, https://budgetlab.yale.edu/research/fiscal-economic-and-distributional-effects-20-tariffs-china-and-25-tariffs-canada-and-mexico#:~:text=The%20tariffs%20reduce%20the%20short,lower%20in%20calendar%20year%202026.

[64] Patrick T. Brown, "Man Does Not Live By Economic Growth Alone," *Public Discourse*, December 3, 2018, https://www.thepublicdiscourse.com/2018/12/47392/.

Cass proposes that we drop the concept of GDP growth as the marker of economic prosperity for Americans. His alternative concept states that since a "labor market in which workers can support strong families and communities is the central determinant of long-term prosperity, [it] should be the central focus of public policy." This gets to the heart of the case for tariffs, as well as for the greater shift in thinking among Republicans from the interests of businesses to the interests of workers and families. A sign of success is when as many Americans as possible have jobs that can support families. If tariffs can bring more of those jobs back to America, then perhaps the more traditional economic markers should take a back seat. Vance is right to reconsider the way we calculate economic prosperity in America.

Critics also worry that protective tariffs will stifle efficiency and innovation because a protected American market that does not have to compete on a fair playing field with other nations will stagnate. Putting aside the fact that the "world market" is not a fair playing field (because there are nations where everything from irresponsible pollution to the ability to pay slave wages provides an unfair advantage), tariffs do not stop competition. Tariffs only create that type of stagnation if the government allows monopolies. Tariffs prevent unfair *foreign* competition. American companies will continue to compete and increase efficiency, productivity, and innovation.

Finally, Vance is acutely aware that reshoring jobs and creating an American manufacturing powerhouse is not just a job-growth and wage-growth strategy. It is also a matter of national security. Reshoring supply chains, especially for critical goods such as food, medicine, weapons, and ammunition, ensures that we are not relying on foreign nations that can shut off the supply in the event of a foreign conflict.[65] Economics aside, it is irresponsible to rely on foreign nations (especially China, who could easily move from a trade partner to a foreign adversary) for the goods America needs to survive and to defend itself.

Between Vance's own actions and the movement within Conservatism to start considering the actual economic position of the average worker (rather than the GDP or the stock market) as the marker of success, we can expect that Vance will continue to guide the Republican Party and the nation toward this way of thinking. Tariffs and creative tax breaks will be a likely tool to focus on good jobs and good wages for as many Americans as possible. That will hopefully become more and more the measure by which Republicans judge good economic policy.

Personnel

"Personnel is policy"[66] has become a cliché for a reason: it is true. The brightest, most strategically brilliant politician on the national stage can do little on his own if his team is not both loyal and competent. This might be the most poignant lesson from President Trump's first term in office. It is impossible for a politician to deliver on implementing a policy platform if his staff is not talented enough to turn campaign promises into effective policies. It is also impossible to deliver if staff members are not aligned on policy priorities, because they will quietly

---

[65] Greg R. Lawson, "Defining the Trump-Vance Doctrine," *The National Interest*, July 30, 2024, https://nationalinterest.org/feature/defining-trump-vance-doctrine-212106.

[66] Jeffrey H. Anderson, "Personnel is Policy," *The American Mind*, October 29, 2024, https://americanmind.org/features/what-trump-should-do-if-he-wins/personnel-is-policy/.

work against their boss. Trump ran on a MAGA platform but did not have the political appointees and bureaucratic staff ready to go on day one to implement his policies. The result was four years of neoconservatives and Liberals working within the DC establishment to stop Trump's agenda from being enacted.

While there were advantages to Trump being an outsider who had never run for political office or held a government position, his outsider status limited his effectiveness. Because he had never run a government office, he did not have the loyalists to staff his administration and prevent his agenda from being undermined. In this case, it is fortunate that Vance is not Trump.

Vance has two important qualities related to his staffing choices. First, he values and receives loyalty. Many of his most intimate advisors and staffers who have been with him since his run for the Senate are still advising and working with him today. This is an asset that many people outside the political world may not understand. The fact that many of Vance's senior staffers and advisors are people he has known and trusted for years is crucial. A politician's friends and confidants are *much* less likely to undermine him. Vance has an inner circle that is incredibly talented in the world of politics and that is fiercely loyal to Vance and his priorities. This is an important indicator that Vance will not suffer from the limitation of the first Trump administration. He has loyal, competent allies who will work for him and ensure that his priorities are implemented rather than undermined.

Second, Vance has a uniquely broad understanding of and relation to the conservative movement in America. Yes, he understands the various theories within American conservatism. He is quite comfortable discussing Catholic integralism, West Coast Straussianism, Libertarianism, National Conservatism, and the dozens of other -isms on the Right. But perhaps more important, he knows and relates to *the people* within these movements. The most talented, intelligent, and patriotic Conservatives throughout this country are affiliated with various movements and organizations. From the Claremont Institute to First Things, Vance knows the people who make up the best and brightest of the conservative movement in this nation. Because Vance is a brilliant thinker, a prolific writer, and an excellent networker, he has made friends and allies among the smartest and most capable Conservatives America has to offer. These alliances are a great asset. As Vance continues to rise as a Republican leader, he will continue to draw the most talented, capable, and loyal people into his orbit from across the spectrum of the conservative movement.

XIV

Conclusion: The Future of the Republican Party Under President Vance?

So back to the questions we started with: Who is JD Vance? And why does it matter?

JD Vance promises to be something that America has not seen in a long time. He is a public intellectual with a fascinating back story who has a deep grasp of the most important policy issues, philosophical currents, and factional disputes facing the conservative movement and the nation at large. He has a clear vision of America as a nation founded on beautiful and unique principles; a place where once strong and healthy institutions have severely decayed; a country that could achieve greatness once more if it focused its government policy on prioritizing strong families and successful workers. And unlike most people in that conservative intellectual world, Vance has the political abilities to be not only a thinker but a political leader.

Vance brings to the table an intellectual track record of intelligent, coherent writings and speeches that show he understands the extent of the problems facing America and the changes required of the Republican Party to address those problems. He brings a compelling story of overcoming adversity and achieving greatness. He possesses one of the greatest intellects among politicians today. And he carries with him a loyal following of political operatives, donors, and conservative intellectuals who will be of great service as he continues to be an American leader and statesman.

Despite the media hysteria attempting to paint Vance as a political extremist, his views and political actions are actually quite balanced. Vance understands the proper role of government, which balances the preference for local institutions and restrained government with a willingness to use government power (where appropriate) for the common good.

He is a devout Catholic and a strong Conservative who is also very prudent. He understands that there are many good policies based on true principles that simply cannot be enacted because the people are not in agreement and will not vote for them.

Vance's political instincts are not reactionary, as are those of many politicians who can feel the change in the political winds and adapt accordingly. Vance has shown a unique habit—one crucial in a leader—of almost prophetically getting to the heart of the matter before it becomes politically popular or obvious. One example is Vance's anti-interventionist foreign policy stances and particularly his opposition to funding the war in Ukraine—Vance was one of the first vocal senators on this issue, before it was cool.

But perhaps a more striking and less obvious example of Vance's prescience is his insight in the speech at the Munich Security Conference, mentioned in the previous chapter. After listing many of the security threats to Europe, Vance warns Europe that the biggest threat to its security is "the threat from within. The retreat of Europe from some of its most fundamental values..."[67]

In the three months after Vance made these comments about Europe endangering itself by retreating from its own values, Marine Le Pen was found guilty of embezzlement by a French court (a conviction she has appealed) and banned from running for office for the next five years—making her ineligible for the next presidential election just as her poll numbers are rising.[68] The German domestic intelligence agency labeled the German right-wing political party "right-wing extremists" and put them under close surveillance.[69] Vance was already focused on a huge global problem in the west, just as it was beginning to erupt. In the name of preserving the liberal regime, the political elites in Europe are undermining core values such as free elections and endangering the peace and stability of their nations. Vance has a knack for putting his finger on central problems, identifying them before they become obvious. This ability to read political situations in real time is a needed asset for a political leader.

---

[67] JD Vance, Speech to Munich Security Conference, *The Spectator*, February 14, 2025, https://thespectator.com/topic/read-jd-vance-full-speech-decay-europe/.
[68] Jack Burgess, "Le Pen Calls Embezzlement Conviction a 'Witch Hunt,'" *BBC*, April 6, 2025, https://www.bbc.com/news/articles/c8dg90l7ymlo.
[69] Nigel Jones, "Labeling the AfD 'extremists' Will Backfire," *The Spectator*, May 2, 2025, https://www.spectator.co.uk/article/labelling-the-afd-extremists-will-backfire-on-its-opponents/.

Frankly, when someone is so brilliant and talented that he can overcome lowly circumstances and become such a successful leader, we should pay close attention. Men like JD Vance are exactly the leaders we need, men who have the talent to lead and the story to inspire the next generation of leaders to overcome the odds and strive for greatness.

Vance's story is not simply about achieving success. It is about the unique type of person he is, someone uniquely situated to lead and guide the Republican Party after Donald Trump. Vance possesses a combination of gifts, talents, and qualities that make him (perhaps more than any other American politician on the Right today) the right person to take up the hard task of defining and leading what the Republican Party will be after 2028. For years, neoconservatism dominated the party. Until Donald Trump, no Republican not named Bush had been president since Reagan. Trump's election showed that the Bush moment was over, that the party had drastically changed. But while the party under Trump has focused on an "America first" emphasis and has prioritized immigration and trade as lead policy issues, it is still not clear exactly what the Republican Party will look like after the uniquely charismatic figure of Donald Trump steps out of the spotlight. JD Vance is the man to lead the party into what comes next.

Why? Unlike many politicians, Vance has been deeply involved in the conservative intellectual movement. The essays and speeches Vance has written over the years show a deep knowledge of not only the political atmosphere in America, but of the different ideas and factions that animate American Conservatism. While Vance is (prudently) not definable by any particular movement or ideology, he has a serious understanding of the different factions that make up the current coalition that is the Republican Party. To hold the party together after Trump, the next Republican leader needs to understand what animates and motivates the neoconservatives and the foreign policy realists. He needs to appreciate the free market and the concept of limited government while being willing to explore proper uses of political power to solve real problems. Very few people among Republican leadership have the intellectual depth and experience to navigate these issues, understand the various factors at play, and help them work together as a coalition rather than descending into intra-party civil war. Vance is the man for the job.

Vance brings with him an incredible political team and the instincts to be able to pick the right people for the right job. Any leader of the Republican Party moving forward will need to ensure that he has the right team of donors, thinkers, and leaders; Vance has a track record of doing just that.

Finally, Vance has something that many political leaders today do not have. He is interesting. His personal story, his ability to handle impromptu questions and engage in fierce debates, and his exceptional political instincts, make for a unique politician. In a world full of stereotypical and forgettable politicians, Vance stands out as someone the voters are actually interested in knowing more about.

So yes, Vance has an incredible intellect, is well-educated, possesses excellent political instincts, and has a host of needed leadership qualities to bring the Republican Party into the post-Trump era. But finally, and perhaps most important, Vance is a normal guy with an inspiring story. He grew up in poverty and dysfunction, learned discipline and maturity in the military, obtained an elite education, and overcame insurmountable odds to become a loving husband and father, a successful professional, and a great politician. Vance has lived the American Dream.

Unlike the many politicians who come from wealth and power and privilege—the American voter has perhaps become a bit bored and tired of Clintons and Bushes going from riches to riches—Vance has a rags-to-riches story that exemplifies what is possible in America. Anyone—even a hillbilly from a chaotic family who struggled from his youth to overcome fatherlessness, poverty, and addiction—can rise. Vance rose. Through hard work, intelligence, study, and a lot of help from a few good people in his community, Vance rose from a kid who was very close to falling through the cracks into the vice president of the United States. JD Vance should reinspire Americans to realize what is possible.

Between Vance's *Hillbilly Elegy* and his extensive body of writing over the last decade, we can do what is almost impossible with the average modern politician. We can put together an extensive profile of who Vance is and what kind of president he would be. While Vance has been unfairly labeled a political opportunist, his writings and speeches reveal a consistent, thoughtful evolution of thought on the state of America (particularly American institutions) and what it would take to fix it. Vance's thought has changed about the state of American institutions between 2016 and the present, but his core political principles and priorities have not. Vance remains essentially concerned with the same problems and possesses the same hope for America that he had in 2016.

Vance and the GOP after Trump will be confirmed as the party of the working man and of the American family. This involves a continued transition toward a new voter base. As the 2024 election showed, the working class (not just the white working class, but a broad coalition including a greater number of black, Hispanic, and Asian voters) have moved to the Republican Party in impressive numbers. This will have to be reinforced by policy priorities that attract and support the working class. As this book demonstrates, Vance's personal background as well as his political views make him the right candidate for this moment. Vance stands ready to re-balance policy priorities away from favoring big corporations and toward small businesses and individual workers. He supports economic policies that return good, working-class manufacturing jobs to the United States from foreign nations and that ensure the average American can provide for a family while doing good, meaningful work.

The platform Vance advocates also prioritizes the formation of stable families. He has signaled an openness to tax policies that favor people getting married and having children. He has been a leader of reining in American foreign policy so our children are not being sent off to fight unnecessary wars.

And while Vance (and the MAGA movement generally) often gets labelled as extreme, most of his thoughts and proposals are actually quite moderate. When families across the country are falling apart by the millions due to job insecurity, drug addiction, community breakdown, and a general loss of hope, the country cannot survive. Vance's responses—considering creative policy ideas on the Right that promote stable marriages and produce more children, push manufacturers to reshore jobs to the US, keep us out of wars that our children will have to fight, and so on—are not extreme. The political priorities Vance articulates might be less libertarian and involve more government action than Republicans are used to promoting, but Vance's diagnosis of the state of affairs in the United States justifies a little less hands-off philosophy and a little more role for government to assist in the solution.

So Vance understands where the Republican Party has been and where it is going. He has navigated a time of great upheaval and change within the Republican Party and in the nation as a whole, and he has done so with almost perfect political instinct. Vance's position as vice president and as Trump's heir apparent, makes him the most likely contender to lead the GOP after Trump. And whether or not Vance becomes the next president, his thought and his politics present a roadmap for the future of the Republican Party. Conservatives, and all those who care about the future of the American family, worker, and nation, should find in Vance the best hope to lead us into the future.

ACKNOWLEDGMENTS

An acknowledgment is a dangerous thing; I am indebted to so many people for this book and for my development as a writer and political commentator in general that I will surely miss most of those who deserve acknowledgment. But I should still try.

To Tom Spence, who supported the idea for this book from day one, taught me everything from how to write a proposal to how forewords work, and made the idea of writing a book seem possible. Tom is one of the kindest and most generous people I have met in this business and I am truly grateful for his friendship.

To Alex Novak and the good folks at Post Hill Press/Bombardier for believing in this idea and helping me along the journey of writing my first book.

To the many editors and writers who have helped me learn how to write over the last few years, particularly Micah Meadowcroft and Jude Russo. Every edit, comment, and (especially) rejected submission has been an invaluable learning experience.

There are too many friends and colleagues to name who have talked through these ideas and supported me. But I can't write an acknowledgment without thanking my dear friend and former colleague, Mary Margaret Bush, for her support and encouragement of me writing this book in my spare time, and for generously reviewing and editing the first sample chapters I drafted.

To Tim Busch and John Peiffer, the co-founders of Napa Legal, for their constant encouragement of my writing endeavors and for helping me so much in my personal and professional life. And to my dear colleagues Helen Rothfus, Joseph Clement, and Andrea Fedrigo, who have patiently listened to my stories and ideas as I put this book together.

And of course, to my dearest wife Molly. I have no idea how she manages to put up with all my eclectic projects, care for and homeschool our five small kids, and still manage to talk through ideas and edit manuscripts for me. Molly, I don't know how you put up with me, manage the household and kids, and manage to be such a loving, supportive, beautiful wife. But thank you; I love you dearly and couldn't imagine doing any of this without you.

ABOUT THE AUTHOR

Frank DeVito is senior counsel and director of content at the Napa Legal Institute. He graduated summa cum laude from Sacred Heart University with a bachelor's degree in philosophy and from Quinnipiac University School of Law. His work has previously been published in *The American Conservative*, *The Federalist*, *Public Discourse*, *The Daily Wire*, *First Things*, *The Claremont Review of Books*, *City Journal*, and several other publications. He is a regular speaker for law school student groups, legal organizations (such as the Federalist Society), and various religious associations and civic groups. He lives in eastern Pennsylvania with his wife and five children.

www.ingramcontent.com/pod-product-compliance
Lightning Source LLC
Chambersburg PA
CBHW070645160426
43194CB00009B/1588